NEW TECHNOLOGIES AND LANGUAGE LEARNING: CASES IN THE LESS COMMONLY TAUGHT LANGUAGES

Stafford Library
Columbia College
1001 Rogers Street
Columbia, Missouri 65216

TECHNICAL REPORT #25

NEW TECHNOLOGIES AND LANGUAGE LEARNING: CASES IN THE LESS COMMONLY TAUGHT LANGUAGES

edited by
CAROL ANNE SPREEN

SECOND LANGUAGE TEACHING & CURRICULUM CENTER
University of Hawai'i at Mānoa

© 2002 Second Language Teaching & Curriculum Center
University of Hawai'i
All rights reserved
Manufactured in the United States of America

The contents of this Technical Report were developed under a grant from the U.S. Department of Education (CFDA 84.229, P229A020002). However, the contents do not necessarily represent the policy of the Department of Education, and one should not assume endorsement by the Federal Government.

ISBN 0–8248–2634–5

♾™ The paper used in this publication meets the minimum requirements of the American National Standard for Information Sciences–Permanence of Paper for Printed Library Materials.

ANSI Z39.48–1984

Book design by Deborah Masterson

Distributed by
University of Hawai'i Press
Order Department
2840 Kolowalu Street
Honolulu, HI 96822–1888

ABOUT THE NATIONAL FOREIGN LANGUAGE RESOURCE CENTER

THE SECOND LANGUAGE TEACHING AND CURRICULUM CENTER of the University of Hawai'i is a unit of the College of Languages, Linguistics and Literature. Under a grant from the U.S. Department of Education, the Center has since 1990 served as a National Foreign Language Resource Center (NFLRC). The general direction of the Resource Center is set by a national advisory board. The Center conducts research, develops materials, and trains language professionals with the goal of improving foreign language instruction in the United States. The Center publishes research reports and teaching materials; it also sponsors summer intensive teacher training institutes. For additional information about Center programs, contact:

Dr. Richard Schmidt, Director
National Foreign Language Resource Center
1859 East-West Road #106
University of Hawai'i
Honolulu, HI 96822–2322

e-mail: nflrc@hawaii.edu
Web site: http://nflrc.hawaii.edu

NFLRC ADVISORY BOARD

Roger Andersen
Applied Linguistics
University of California, Los Angeles

Kathleen Bardovi-Harlig
Program for TESOL and Applied Linguistics
Indiana University

Carol Chapelle
English Department
Iowa State University

Dorothy Chun
Department of Germanic, Slavic, & Semitic Studies
University of California at Santa Barbara

John Clark
Defense Language Institute (Emeritus)
Monterey, California

James Pusack
Department of German
University of Iowa

CONTENTS

About the National Security Education Program ix

Preface xiii

Models for Distance Education in Critical Languages
David Hiple & Stephen Fleming 1

Foreign Language Distance Education:
The University of Hawai'i Experience
Stephen Fleming, David Hiple, & Yun Du 13

Language Learning and the Internet:
Student Strategies in Vocabulary Acquisition
Rhodalyne Gallo-Crail & Robert Zerwekh 55

Video in the Virtual Language Class:
Building a Model for Web-Based Instruction
Ken Petersen 81

The Impact of Self-Instructional Technology on Language Learning:
A View of NASILP
Alexander Dunkel, Scott Brill, & Bryan Kohl 97

LangMedia, a World Wide Web Site for Language and Culture,
and the Role of International Students in Its Creation
Elizabeth H. D. Mazzocco 121

A New Paradigm for Less Commonly Taught Languages:
The Arabic Language and Middle East/North
African Cultural Studies Program
Norman J. Peterson 135

About the Contributors 145

ABOUT THE NATIONAL SECURITY EDUCATION PROGRAM

The National Security Education Program (NSEP) is the result of the David L. Boren National Security Education Act of 1991. The objective of the NSEP is to enhance the national security of the US by increasing our capacity to deal effectively with less-commonly taught languages and cultures. The NSEP consists of three initiatives established by the legislation: (1) scholarships to U.S. undergraduate students to study abroad in world areas critical to U.S. national security; (2) fellowships to U.S. graduate students to study, in the U.S. and abroad, foreign languages, disciplines, and/or geographic areas that will strengthen U.S. national security; and (3) grants to U.S. institutions of higher education (or consortia led by such institutions) to establish and/or improve programs in critical but less-commonly studied foreign languages and world regions, together with a focus on fields of study critical to U.S. national security. Integral to the NSEP is the objective to produce a pool of highly-skilled professional applicants for work in the federal government with national security responsibilities who will make effective U.S. policy.

Initiated in Fall 2000, NSEP formed a technology working group and invited six programs to research their practices and develop case studies (compiled in this edited volume) across a diverse set of languages and technological approaches. The NSEP-funded university programs and associated languages included in this compilation are Montana State University and UW (Arabic); Northern Illinois University (Thai, Indonesian, Vietnamese, Tagalog); Indiana University and the American Council for International Education (Azeri, Kazakh, Turkmen, Uzbek, Hungarian); University of Hawai'i at Mānoa (Chinese); Five Colleges Incorporated (Bulgarian, Brazilian Portuguese, Czech, Hindi, Hungarian, Indonesian); and the National Association of Self-Instructional Language at the University of Arizona (Korean, Turkish, Mandarin Chinese, Cantonese, Brazilian Portuguese, Kazakh, and other less commonly taught languages).

This book describes the current use and limitations of different forms of technology in language instruction funded through the NSEP Institutional Grants program. The compilation of case studies explores the impact of technology on less-commonly taught languages. These case studies will help identify the strengths as well as shortcomings of new technologies and related pedagogies and disseminate findings that will help guide and inform technology use for language instruction in higher education institutions.

Contact information for the NSEP:
Robert O. Slater, Director
National Security Education Program
1101 Wilson Boulevard, Suite 1210
Arlington, VA 22209-2246
703-696-1991
Or please visit our Web site at www.ndu.edu/nsep

PARTICIPATING UNIVERSITIES AND ORGANIZATIONS

National Association for Self-Instructional Language Programs
University of Arizona
1717 E. Speedway Blvd. Suite 3312
Tucson, AZ 85721–0151
http://nasilp.org
contact: Alex Dunkel, Director
adunkel@u.arizona.edu
phone: 520–626–9209

Second Language Teaching and Curriculum Center
National Foreign Language Resource Center
1859 East-West Road #106
University of Hawai'i at Mānoa
Honolulu, HI 96822–2322
http://www.nflrc.hawaii.edu
contact: David Hiple, Director
dhiple@hawaii.edu
phone: 808–956–2062

Foreign Language Resource Center/Five Colleges
Department of French and Italian Studies
Herter Hall, 161 Presidents Drive
University of Massachusetts
Amherst, MA 01003–9312
http://langmedia.fivecolleges.edu
contact: Elizabeth Mazzocco
mazzocco@frital.umass.edu
phone: 413–545–3453

Center for Southeast Asian Studies
Northern Illinois University
412 Adams Hall
DeKalb, Illinois 60115–3071
http://www.seasite.niu.edu
contact: Bob Zerwekh
zerwekh@cs.niu.edu
phone: 815–753–1771

American Council for International Education
ACIE/ACTR
1776 Massachusetts Ave, NW Suite 700
Washington, DC 20036-1911
http://actr.org
contact: Ken Petersen
kpeter@actr.org
phone: 202-833-7522

Inner Asian and Uralic National Resource Center
Indiana University
Goodbody Hall 157
Bloomington, IN 47405-2401
http://www.cenasianet.org
contact: Bill Fierman
wfierman@indiana.edu
phone: 812-856-5263

Arabic Language and Middle East/North African Cultural Studies Program
Montana State University — Bozeman
400 Culbertson Hall
Bozeman, MT 59717-0001
http://www.montana.edu/international
contact: Norm Peterson
normp@montana.edu
phone: 406-994-7150

PREFACE

This Technical Report includes eight papers that were presented at a working group meeting at the University of Washington in September 2001, sponsored by the National Security Education Program (NSEP). The NSEP invited seven universities funded through the Institutional Grant Program to develop a series of case studies on technology and language learning. The working group represented a range of higher education institutions and related organizations across a diverse set of languages using different technological approaches. These cases represent many of the themes and issues confronted when technology-based instruction, or e-language, is used in language programs throughout the higher education community. The following case studies have been written to identify the strengths as well as the shortcomings of new technologies and related pedagogies particularly for teaching the less-commonly taught languages (LCTLs).

In recent years, an increasing number of programs and proposals for teaching the LCTLs using different technological media have been submitted to the NSEP. Upon awarding a number of these grants, we wondered how to assist in supporting these unique programs, as well as how to evaluate their effectiveness. An extensive literature search produced few results. By bringing together individuals and groups that were working with a variety of aspects of technology and different languages it was our hope that we could share experiences and knowledge and determine a research agenda that would inform and guide the field.

This compilation offers many of the lessons learned on the ground, how decisions and choices were made, how mistakes were corrected, and how project staff aimed at a moving target as the technology changed and learning applications became more complex. We offer these cases not to endorse a particular program, promote a specific software or delivery system, or to sell a product. Instead we hope to present a range of options (as well as describe some of their limitations) that will help faculty and universities make more informed decisions about language programming and technology.

OVERVIEW OF CHAPTERS

The following set of cases begin to describe different types of technologies that are used to support language programs (i.e., Web- or ITV-based, and/or audio/video instructional materials) and to help identify what, if any, are the identifiable trends for instructional technologies. They also describe how technology addresses issues of equity (in terms of under-served or under-represented students), issues of diversity (in terms of access to a broader range of language programs in a wider distribution of institutions), and flexibility (times available and accessibility to students).

Chapter 1 provides an overview of the technological landscape, describing and defining the evolution of key terms and characteristics of different instructional technologies. The authors elaborate on the types and uses of different technologies and their cognitive implications. Finally, they lay out where the future trends are and suggest where distributed learning is likely to go in the foreseeable future.

In chapter 2, the authors more closely examine foreign language distance education with a case study of Web-based courses and assessment processes for teaching beginning and intermediate Chinese at the University of Hawai'i at Mānoa. It presents research findings illustrating the instruments and procedures for developing and evaluating Web-based learning environments, performance-based learning experiences, and language competency.

Chapter 3 describes the results of a semester long study that was conducted with 20 students studying Tagalog at Northern Illinois University (NIU). SEAsite (www.seasite.niu.edu) is an Internet site which offers interactive learning resources for Southeast Asian languages, literatures, and cultures. Developed at NIU, SEAsite currently offers beginning and intermediate language instruction in Thai, Indonesian, Tagalog, and Vietnamese. The case study specifically was interested in assessing how these students used different learning strategies with different Web-based tools as they studied new vocabulary words and how this affected their success in learning and mastering the new second language vocabulary. Results of the case study indicate that students who use a variety of learning strategies achieved a higher level of word mastery and retention than those who used only a few of the available strategies.

Chapter 4 examines the technological and pedagogical considerations that shaped the production of the CenAsiaNet Web-based video modules, piloted at Indiana University. CenAsiaNet is intended as a resource for educators and curriculum developers who would like to utilize the potential of the Internet, but are overwhelmed by the array of questions that arise with the endeavor. By detailing the many choices made by the CenAsiaNet team, it offers an example of how to implement an Internet-based approach to material design for language instruction.

NASILP serves as the largest and oldest national forum for the interchange of ideas and expertise toward the development and support of self-instructional academic curricula for the LCTLs. With support from the NSEP, NASILP has worked with a consortium of academic units to develop four technologically oriented projects including the Critical Languages Series™ (CLS) of CD-ROM sets for six LCTLs; the MaxAuthor™, dedicated to the production of language materials for CD-ROM and the Internet; LCTL FAQ pages for Internet delivery, addressing language-specific questions frequently asked by both students and teachers; and the Internet delivery of hyper textual multimedia informational resources to students, tutors, examiners, and coordinators working with the NASILP system. This case study in chapter 5 is devoted to identifying the impact of these technological innovations on the teaching and learning of LCTLs in the United States.

The Five College Foreign Language Resource Center's development of Web-based, multimedia materials to supplement the study of language and culture relies on its fleet of international students to shoot appropriate video in the target country. They used this method in designing their NSEP-funded Web site, LangMedia. Chapter 6 will examine the impetus for the site, the decisions that went into its design, and the integral role played by international students in the overall construction of LangMedia.

Finally, in a project developed by Montana State University-Bozeman in cooperation with the University of Washington and Al Akhawayn University in Morocco, chapter 7 discusses how to combine resources in an inter-university consortium to make LCTL education more affordable and enable their more continual and frequent offering.

APPROACHES TO LESS COMMONLY TAUGHT LANGUAGES IN HIGHER EDUCATION

In light of the recent tragic events in the United States, there can be little debate that the era of globalization has brought increasingly diverse and complex challenges to our national security. There has been a dramatic revisiting of our capacity to effectively deal with evolving economic and political changes at the global, regional, and local levels. With this renewed reflection comes an increasing demand for professional expertise and leadership bolstered by a broad mix of international skills, including the ability to communicate and understand the languages and cultures of key world regions.

Increasingly, higher education institutions have recognized the importance of their role as the leaders of innovation and change as trainers and educators for the society of the twenty-first century. In recent years, faculty and administrators have begun to embrace the challenge by expanding interdisciplinary curriculum and creating new courses that internationalize programs and disciplines. They have also worked to integrate new learning technologies into the classroom and expanding opportunities for distance education. The higher education community has also become more attuned to the practical skills needed by its graduates to meet the demands of living in a global society by creating opportunities for partnerships with government and industry. Clearly, in our inter-connected world there is an increased need for students to develop international skills — essential to these skills are competencies in area and language knowledge.

Now more than ever before, there are increased demands for language competent professionals across a variety of disciplines, with the ability to communicate in everyday, culturally appropriate interactions. Moreover, the recent tragedies underscore the need for language and cultural skills in areas outside of Western Europe. These growing and changing needs for foreign language competency, especially in the "low-density" or less-commonly taught languages have resulted in a large scale efforts to rethink language programming, both in terms of which languages are offered and at what levels. However, the general problem of low enrollments, limited access, and high costs of teaching LCTLs are critical issues for language faculty and higher education administrators. For nearly a decade, the imperative of the NSEP has been to seek partnerships with higher education institutions to develop an infrastructure to enhance language acquisition in the LCTLs as well as higher levels of language competency as part of its overall mission.

As we move ahead to explore the development of an institutional infrastructure for LCTLs, we must confront a number of important questions: What are the goals and purposes of these language programs? What are the most effective learning environments for teaching uncommonly-taught foreign languages? Which pedagogical tools are most effective and what are the technical issues for designing their delivery systems? What are the different considerations for designing interactive, distributed, and or stand-alone language resources? How can we design courses and select curriculum materials to address the broad range of language skills — including speaking, reading, listening, and writing — needed to operate effectively in a global environment?

Research in second-language acquisition and learning has been carried out for over a century, more recently yielding important knowledge about the way different language learners acquire language proficiencies. In terms of language instruction, there has been a distinct shift away from the more traditional approach to language instruction — based on grammar and syntax — to a more eclectic approach emphasizing communicative competence or fluency. There is a general lack of well-designed studies that identify and control for the multiple variables that influence language acquisition (namely learning environments, instructional approaches, individual and group differences, and differences across languages). Studies that do exist generally fail to address differences across levels and types of language instruction and are limited by small sample sizes. The high investment in time and resources needed to carry out longitudinal or impact studies on language competency has also hindered research efforts in this area (e.g., the Department of Education proposal for the extensive research on distributed learning by SEAsite [http://www.seasite.niu.edu] highlights this concern).

As previously mentioned, due to low enrollments and high costs, most institutions are unwilling to offer courses in the less-commonly taught languages, and for most students only the commonly taught languages are generally available as standard, classroom-formatted instructional programs. In response to this shortfall, many institutions opt for technology-based language programs for the LCTLs because they are perceived to be highly cost-effective instructional solutions. Hence, technologically based language programs represent the only opportunity for language instruction in many languages and the only access to second-language learning for students at remote locations. Consequently, there has been a growing demand for teaching materials and instructional resources that allow students to develop and maintain proficiencies in the LCTLs. Yet, this development of new pedagogies and application of new instructional technologies raises new sets of issues about their effectiveness in meshing with traditional classroom practice.

There is a paucity of research explaining or predicting phenomena related to language acquisition through technology. Research in computer-aided or technologically based language learning has a shorter history and a more complicated set of research problems than traditional language methods. For example, most studies are limited to students in a particular university using custom software in a particular learning environment, whereas these conditions are impossible to control for in online, Web-based, or ITV-based programs. A review of the literature suggests that there are very few qualitative or ethnographic research studies, and even fewer quantitative analyses, of the relationship between technology and language acquisition. The effectiveness of various second language teaching methods has long been debated, as have concerns over how, where, when, and in what order learning activities should take place. Most instead emphasize the broad reaching research on technology and learning processes. Our concern is more limited but equally important; our case studies are designed to discover ways in which different technologies have been used in university settings to teach a variety of languages at different levels of competency.

NSEP'S CASE STUDY INITIATIVE ON LANGUAGE LEARNING AND TECHNOLOGY

To understand the limitations and capabilities afforded by new technologies and language learning, NSEP is supporting research and development to describe and evaluate the current state of the field and develop clear benchmarks for progress. We have used the following key issues to frame the overall objectives of the case study research: identifying the different forms of technology used in existing language programs, descriptive explanations of the ways technology is used to support and enhance language learning, assessment and/or evaluation of different forms of language media and their applicability with a variety of languages in multiple settings and levels, analysis of the required resources (both material and physical) and an examination of "cost-effectiveness" of technology-based instruction, and finally, the development of "benchmarks" or indicators that can be used by faculty or institutions to consider the format and type of technology to support new language programs. Specifically, the case studies were created to answer the following questions:

1. *What are the current instructional technologies used in language programs and who are they used by?* What are the current forms of technology used in language programming at universities in the United States? (For example, are they ITV, Web-based, or via video/audio instructional materials? Are these part of collaborative or consortial arrangements, and if so how are resources shared?

2. *What are some of the primary uses for technology in language programs?* How is technology used? Is it a primary instructional delivery system? Is it supplemental to a traditional language classroom? Is it used as part of a distance learning program? What types of infrastructural support and distribution mechanisms are used?

3. *How do we assess and evaluate language competency?* Which technologies are most appropriate at different levels (beginning, intermediate, advanced) of learning? What kinds of materials are most appropriately covered through language mediated uses of technology?

4. *How do we measure resources, support, and costs of e-language learning?* What resources are required to develop, implement, and maintain technologically based language programs? What are the costs? What time is required for training/faculty development and support/tech support/etc.? How does this compare with traditional language instruction?

5. *What are the benchmarks for technologically based language programs?* How is language competency measured? What are the different assessment tools? How does this approach address issues of equity (in terms of under-served or under-represented students), issues of diversity (in terms of access to a broader range of language programs in a wider distribution of institutions), and flexibility (times available and accessibility to students)? What is the attrition rate and what are the explanations given?

These broad research parameters are important because they provide both descriptive and quantitative analysis of language programming in higher education that can inform the field and help make policy recommendations about new ways to address and increase our national language capacity.

With the wide range of expertise in language pedagogy, instructional technology and program development that has been supported in each of these NSEP-funded programs, we hope the research supported by this framework will generate further comments and a lively discussion in the international education and foreign language fields. Each of the individual case studies addresses different aspects of the research questions. The purpose here is to map out the landscape of the major issues and concerns in this area, and then explore the "fit" or lessons learned for developing other programs. We strongly encourage you to contact the authors or our office to comment on or add to the ideas presented in this edited compilation.

PROMISES AND PITFALLS OF TECHNOLOGY IN LANGUAGE LEARNING

The issue of successful technology-based strategies for second language learning is wide open for exploration. E-language (as it is sometimes known) learning is here and growing. Obviously a number of design and implementation issues factor into the learning environment. These range from attitudes of the learners, study habits, types of activities provided, and the time and willingness of users to participate on tasks. We also know that a variety of components are available to support language instruction — including culturally situated exercises and projects, authentic materials and experiences (especially audio and video), methods that appeal to a variety of individual learning styles and abilities, and everyday or authentic interactions that address real information needs of learners. Yet, how do we begin to address these in an electronic learning environment? Through access to Web sites, audio/video materials, and interactive television, new forms of technology afford the luxury of making available a variety of "realia" in remote learning environments. It also accommodates the learner by providing the information in a variety of formats, as individual learners vary in their skills, background, and language backgrounds. It enables individuals who may vary in their skills to come to a learning activity and complete it at their own pace, possibly accessing additional resources if needed. Finally, e-language enables additional informal forms of communication through e-mail, chatrooms, discussion forums, newsgroups, and teleconferencing that help enhance fluency and expand language use. New forms of technology in all their diversity offer a wide range of learning opportunities for second language learners. The task of course is navigating these resources and creating optimal learning environments.

GUIDING QUESTIONS: MAPPING THE LANDSCAPE OF E-LANGUAGE LEARNING

1. *What are the current instructional technologies used in language programs and who are they used by?*

Our first area of concern centers on the different forms of technology used as a medium of instruction in higher education and who are the target audiences. A study by the National Education Association (NEA, 2000) on distance learning revealed the following: distance learning faculty and traditional faculty teach courses in the same academic fields; 82% of distance learning courses are at the undergraduate level, while 16% are at the graduate level; 70% of the courses fulfill a requirement, while 20% are an elective course; and of those institutions offering distance education, at least 58% used Internet-based courses, 54% used two-way interactive video, and 47% used one-way pre-recorded video.

Also according to the NEA study (2000), Web-based distance education faculty rated their courses better than traditional courses in the following areas: access to information, high quality course material, mastering subject matter, assessing educational effectiveness of the course, and addressing the variety of student learning styles. Faculty rated distance learning courses the same as a traditional course in improving quantitative skills and developing student interactivity. They believe distance learning will reach many students who cannot take traditional college courses and that smaller institutions will be able to offer a richer curriculum, especially Web-based programs because most can occur at any time and any place. Finally, the Web-based faculty rated their distance learning courses worse than a traditional course in strengthening students' group problem-solving skills and helping students deliver oral presentations.

These figures counter some of the expectations that distance learning courses are emerging disproportionately in selected areas of study. In another example, a study conducted by the Council for Higher Education Accreditation (CHEA), revealed that at both 2- and 4-year institutions a trend in distance education is to increase the number of courses using asynchronous computer-based technology (or Web-based applications) as opposed to offering courses that use one-way or two-way video. (CHEA, 2000, p. 2). Identifying these trends in the context of language programming can begin to provide a framework for understanding more complex issues about program development, support and institutionalization. Through the current available technology many language programs are now available to wider audiences in different locations, with different education and language experiences, and different learning expectations. As we will see in the following chapters, which technologies are used and how they are used has several pedagogical considerations.

2. *What are some of the primary uses for technology in language programs?*

Our second area of interest is how technology is used. Whether as part of a primary instructional delivery system or integrated with other programs as supplemental to a traditional language classroom or part of a distance learning program, the use and application of technology will impact differently on language pedagogy and ultimately on language acquisition. The literature points to an important distinction between the different forms of technology as language-based technology and non-language-based technology (Salaberry, 2000). The former is designed specifically for language-related tasks, and includes speech recognition and synthesis, lemmatization, syntactic categorization, vocabulary extraction, parsing, and text generation. As some of the following case studies illustrate, addressing technical issues such as selecting hardware or software is of critical importance for program design and pedagogical implications. The cases discuss their decision-making processes behind their selections and the applicability of different hardware/software, especially in working with other fonts and numerals.

The latter (which is complementary, but not as exclusive) includes hypertext, digital audio and video, database technology, and networked communication. It is also of interest to know whether and how technology is used to enhance cultural awareness (i.e., Is using video beneficial in providing visual images of behaviors, and as a result does it increase the awareness of local values and culture that are not available through text?). And if so, how it is used increase access to broader, interdisciplinary information (such as geopolitical concerns or primary source materials)?

Another issue that has arisen through the case study examples is whether a trend exists toward integrating multiple computing or technological resources. While not endorsing a particular software or hardware application, these and other similar figures on trends in technology-based language learning offer insight into the "how" and "why" of language programming, as well as address some of the benefits and limitations of one approach over another.

3. *How do we assess and evaluate language competency?*

One question driving the case studies was which technologies are most appropriate for which levels of instruction? Hence, case studies start to answer how language competency is measured, what different assessment tools are available, and whether or how text, sound, video, or any combinations of these have proved more effective in language acquisition.

Several of the case studies focus on the assessment and evaluation of learning and measurement indicators for how different technologies impact on language development. While it seems straightforward that different applications and exercises would benefit learners at different ability levels in different ways, how individuals with a variety of skill levels can use the same applications is unclear. In addition, mutually agreed upon (or externally measured) language competency indicators are a relatively new and unpracticed concept in most language programs. Few examples of language measurement instruments exist, especially for the LCTLs, and those that do are often expensive and have a relatively small pay-off. To remedy this oversight the development of a variety of examples of different forms of assessment or guidance on evaluation of technologically based language programs can help in their development and improvement.

4. *How do we measure resources, support, and costs of e-language learning?*

A fourth area centers on the resources and cost effectiveness of developing, implementing, and maintaining technologically based language programs. Most universities are seeking a cost-effective instructional format to offer LCTLs on a regular basis to a very small number of students. However, despite the assumption that using technology lowers costs and increases access, current developers and users assert that technologically based and distance education is often more expensive than a comparable traditional course.

A study on distance education done by the Institute for Higher Education Policy (NEA, 2000) found that many faculty worried that they would suffer financially because persons teaching distance education courses are likely to do more work for the same amount of pay and because they are not fairly compensated for their intellectual property. They also felt they would have to spend more time mastering the procedural as well as the declarative knowledge to teach languages through technology. In terms of demanding more time from faculty, 53% of those actually teaching a distance learning course reported spending more hours per week preparing and delivering it and in spite of spending longer hours preparing and presenting, 84% said they receive no course reduction for their work, and 63% are compensated as if their distance learning course were part of their normal course load (NEA 2000, p. 50). Costs are also incurred by faculty requiring training in the use of new technologies and by institutions requiring technical support and infrastructure maintenance.

Issues of cost and extra time spent in preparing for and teaching distance learning courses raise concerns over faculty incentives and recognition of the additional work that goes into preparing and teaching remotely. In fact, most DL courses are taught by technology savvy junior faculty, and at present, the academic reward system does not take into consideration their extra time, effort, and expertise when it comes time for promotion and tenure. The issue of incentivizing faculty to teach DL courses (because of their potential to reach a broader range of students and their ability to increase the level and types of languages universities offer), should be given greater thought in higher education planning.

In addition to the expenses incurred by the training and maintenance of technologically apt faculty, there are high attrition rates in LCTL programs resulting in weak return of language expertise. In spite of the huge technological investments incurred to develop tech-based programs at certain levels of language instruction, in most LCTLs, students drop out by the third year of study. For example, approximately 75% of students beginning Russian will drop out by the third year of study (Brecht, Caemmerer, & Walton, 1995). Based on the literature, one can conclude that the bulk of resources in Russian programs are directed to the general education mission, where there are little applied or language specialization skills. When it comes to allocating resources and evaluating the return on the investment for supporting instructional technology, these issues weigh in heavily on decisions to support or establish programs for LCTLs.

Much of the research suggests that the greatest benefit of technology in language acquisition is through the collaborative development of resources, and that benefits are realized in the area of those languages for which there is a significant demand, but which have insufficient numbers of students (i.e., the less-commonly taught languages, special purpose courses in common languages such as business Russian, and highly specialized advanced courses; Symposium on Technology and Foreign Language Learning, 1996). Inter-university or interdepartmental collaboration demands that institutions share technological resources, and establish the infrastructure and mechanisms for archiving, organization, and dissemination processes. Hence, a few of the case studies in this compilation have identified the specific infrastructural support, collaborative, and distribution mechanisms that different institutions have chosen to utilize.

5. *What are the benchmarks for technologically based language programs?*

The last area of concern centered on the development, institutionalization, and evaluation of technology-based language programs. According to current understanding, the benchmarks for institutionalizing and also evaluating a language program must include and measure the following:

- Institutional support: infrastructure issues, technology plan
- Course development: design, delivery, technology used
- Teaching/learning: pedagogy, student interaction with faculty, feedback to students
- Course structure: course objectives, library resources, student expectations
- Student support: admissions, financial aid
- Faculty support: assist in transition from classroom teaching to online instruction

Hence, the challenge put forth by these case studies is to establish which technologies are commonly used and which are best suited to specific areas of second language teaching (such as speaking, vocabulary, grammar, reading, writing, and assessment) and by whom. Some of these case studies start to shed light on ways to target public resources to the poorest beneficiaries, enabling poor or under-served students to overcome the cost and time barriers to language learning. Based on the issues that were briefly introduced above, we hope the case studies will begin to clarify where and how technology is used to teach languages (i.e., in what fields of study, levels and types of languages, and whether for required or elective courses) and to help illustrate whether and how these applications are successful.

CONCLUSION

As a government-based grant-giving organization in this era of concern about program effectiveness we felt that criteria for organizing and measuring language programs and disseminating their results should be established. In order to explain how technology addresses issues of equity, diversity, and flexibility in language programming, important indicators should be considered by anyone investing in technology for language programs. Our collective experience pushed us to include and address the following questions in the case studies: Are costs prohibitive for a substantial number of students? Is technology defeating or supporting our effort to increase access by reaching a more diverse set students? Are students who are using technology or learning at a distance disadvantaged by in terms of quality of content, input and delivery, are there other factors that support or impede their learners compared to their peers in traditional classrooms? Are there data suggesting that these students fare as well or better if they use these non-traditional learning methods? Are there only a few language communities or certain types of institutions that can offer computer and Internet access, highly competent teachers, self-guided curricula, and so forth to students? Finally, what are the success rates of these programs, how is effectiveness measured and what are the explanations given?

BIBLIOGRAPHY

Bradley, T., & Lomicka, L. (1999, July). Review of new ways of learning and teaching: Focus on technology and foreign language education. *Language Learning & Technology, 3*(1). Retrieved July 19, 2000, from: http://llt.msu.edu/vol3num1/review/review2.html.

The American Center for the Study of Distance Education, Research Symposia and Conference, Penn State College of Education, Retrieved July 19, 2000, from: http://www.ed.psu.edu/acsde/conferences/symp.asp

Brecht, R. D., with Caemmerer, J., & Walton, R. A. (1995). *Russian in the United States: A case study of America's language needs and capacities*, National Foreign Language Center Monograph Series. Baltimore: Johns Hopkins University.

Council for Higher Education Accreditation. (2000). *Distance Learning in Higher Education*, CHEA Number 3. Retrieved July 26, 2000, from: http://www.chea.org/Commentary/distance-learning-3.cfm

Institute for Higher Education Policy. (1999, April). *What's the difference? A review of contemporary research on the effectiveness of distance learning in higher education.* National Education Association.

Institute for Higher Education Policy. (2000, April). *Quality on the line: Benchmarks for success in Internet-based distance education.* National Education Association.

Jeffries, M. *IPSE-Research in Distance Education.* Retrieved July 19, 2000, from: http://www.ihets.org/consortium/ipse/fdhandbook/resrch.html

Kasper, L. F. (1999, July). Review of electronic literacies: Language, culture and power in online education by Mark Warschauer. In *Language Learning & Technology, 3*(1). Retrieved July 19, 2000, from: http://llt.msu.edu/vol3num1/review3.html

National Education Association. (2000, June). A Survey of Traditional and Distance Learning Higher Education Members Commissioned by the Education Association, Washington, www.nea.org/he

Salaberry, R. (2000, May). Review of Language Teaching and Technology. *Language Learning & Technology, 4*(1), pp. 22–25. Retrieved July 19, 2000, from: http://llt.msu.edu/vol4num1/review2/default.html

Symposium on Technology and Foreign Language Learning. (1996, March 8–10). Ohio State University. Retrieved July 19, 2000, from: http://www.cic.uiuc.edu/resources/langsym/finalrpt.html

Teaching with the Web. Retrieved July 19, 2000, from: http://polyglot.lss.wisc.edu/lss/lang/teach/teachlink.html

NEW TECHNOLOGIES AND LANGUAGE LEARNING: CASES IN THE LESS COMMONLY TAUGHT LANGUAGES

David Hiple & Stephen Fleming
University of Hawai'i at Mānoa

MODELS FOR DISTANCE EDUCATION IN CRITICAL LANGUAGES

EVOLVING DEFINITION OF DISTANCE EDUCATION

Distance education has been defined differently at different points in history. Traditional or conservative definitions of distance education refer only to a separation between teacher and learner and their use of some means of communication. Such broadly based definitions are of limited utility in the Information Age, since they could apply equally to a correspondence course conducted by post in the 1920s or to a workshop conducted via synchronous Web-based videoconferencing in 2001. As communications technology has evolved from paper and pencil through radio, television, and the Internet, the definition of distance education has changed accordingly, so that newer definitions of distance education have come to include additional criteria. For example, Keegan (1990) suggests that distance education has the following characteristics:

- separation of a teacher and learner throughout the learning process;
- separation of the learner or learners from other learners or learning groups;
- provision of means for two-way communication so that the learner(s) can benefit from or initiate dialogue; and
- utilization of electrical means of communication to carry the content of the course.

In this definition, Keegan has articulated two important features that have come to distinguish distance education in the Information Age: first, in addition to the separation between teacher and learner, communication must be *electronically based*; second, communication must be *bi-directional*. Not only does the student receive communication from the teacher; the student also directs communication to the teacher and to other students.

DISTANCE EDUCATION AND L2/FL INSTRUCTION

Keegan's bi-directional criterion deserves special emphasis in the context of second and foreign language instruction. In the past few decades, specialists in language pedagogy have increasingly come to recognize that language is more a complex set of interdependent skills or competencies than a body of mastered knowledge

---

Hiple, D., & Fleming, S. (2002). Models for distance education in critical languages. In C. A. Spreen (Ed.), *New technologies and language learning: Cases in the less commonly taught languages* (Technical Report #25; pp. 1–11). Honolulu, HI: University of Hawai'i, Second Language Teaching & Curriculum Center.

(Omaggio Hadley, 2001). This recognition has been reflected in two important areas. First of all, evaluation of learners' competence in a language increasingly focuses on their ability to perform communicative tasks rather than manipulate linguistic forms. Secondly, classroom practices increasingly emphasize the use of actual communication in language learning activities while de-emphasizing the mastery of language metaknowledge, for example, rules of phonology and syntax. In light of this shift, the criterion that distance education media must enable bi-directional communication takes on special importance for language instruction applications. Information Age forms of distance education, due to their interactive nature, are better suited to language instruction. Forms of distance education that do not fit the Information Age criteria cannot fulfill the communicative requirements of modern language instruction.

HISTORICAL EVOLUTION OF DISTANCE EDUCATION DELIVERY MODES

Early in distance education history, paper-and-pencil correspondence was the only means for the transmission of information between teacher and student. Learners engaged in self-instructional home study of course materials, then submitted assignments and/or tests to the course instructor by post. This postal traffic passed slowly in two directions and was certainly not electronic. For these reasons, early correspondence courses offered in the past through such institutions as Great Britain's Open University do not fit the Information Age definition of distance education. (Note: The Open University now offers electronically tutored courses.)

As communications technology advanced, radio and television made the means of transmission electronic, but allowed only one-way delivery of instruction from teacher to student. The lack of an interactive element in such television-based courses as those of NYU's Sunrise Semester (ca. 1950s–1980s) means that courses of this type also do not fit the Information Age definition of distance education.

The advent of interactive television (ITV) technology made it possible to link learners at multiple locations into a single virtual classroom through video and voice transmission, meeting the Information Age imperative of electronically-based communicative interaction. ITV thus became the first form of distance education to meet the criteria of the Information Age definition of distance education.

In the 1960s, the development of computer-assisted instruction (CAI), which includes computer-assisted language learning (CALL), focused on the capability of the computer as "teaching machine" to provide stimulus and feedback to the learner (Saettler, 1990). Before the advent of networking, however, computers could not serve as tools of communication, and so in its classic form one software user on one machine, CALL did not represent a form of distance education at all, but rather a form of self-instruction or independent learning.

Only when universal availability of e-mail and the Web in the 1990s enabled the creation of virtual classrooms in cyberspace did computer-based forms of instruction become bi-directionally communicative. As of this writing, while Internet applications such as e-mail and Multi-User Object-Oriented Environments (MOOs) are still in use, the World Wide Web has completely overshadowed them as a platform for the delivery of distance education.

In the Information Age, ITV and the Internet — especially the Web — have come to dominate the distance education scene. The relative costs and benefits of these two media are discussed below.

INTERACTIVE TELEVISION (ITV)

Among technologies available for distance education, ITV offers the closest replication of the traditional classroom. The face-to-face communication it enables yields particular advantages for teaching listening/speaking to language learners. In fact, it is hard to see how language could be effectively taught at the beginning levels in the absence of such face-to-face interaction. However, ITV is an extremely capital-intensive technology requiring massive investment usually at the state or system level and has geographical limitations as well.

An ITV system serves a limited number of specialized classroom sites linked by special transmission technology. These classrooms are usually located on separate campuses within a large institution such as a state educational network or a state university system. While the system generally serves locations that are geographically remote enough from one another to render commuting impractical, users must still be physically present in an ITV classroom; they cannot study from home.

Typically, a single ITV class does not include more than three or four remote-site locations in addition to the originating site. Moreover, ITV is a synchronous or "live" technology, requiring the presence of everyone in the classroom at the same time. The requirement for fixed class meeting times and the expense of transmitting television signals outside a single system mean that ITV cannot practically and efficiently serve learners across institutional boundaries and across multiple time zones on an ongoing basis. Therefore, while ITV does offer particular educational advantages, it is chiefly an *intercampus* course-delivery system and does not offer global accessibility.

In the context of language instruction, it appears that ITV-based distance education offers the strongest advantages for the teaching of languages in which learners are widely scattered on the ground but still within the single large institution served by the ITV network. Learners at several sites can be gathered together to form a class where previously none was feasible. This means that ITV can help preserve four-skill, first- and second-year instruction in less commonly taught languages in large, multi-campus institutions in which they might otherwise suffer cancellation.

APPLYING THE ITV MODEL ACROSS SYSTEMS

The technology of ITV systems varies considerably from institution to institution, and these differences, though small, may constrain instructors' choices in important ways. A short summary of these differences follows.

Video quality in ITV systems transmitting compressed video over ISDN (Integrated Services Digital Network) lines varies widely, but even the highest quality ISDN is not as clear as full-motion video. In terms of instructional strategies, this would mean that any activity depending on video clarity, such as reading on screen or distinguishing visual characteristics of an on-screen object or person, would have to be used with due caution.

Many ITV systems are videoconferencing systems, some of which are more limited than others. In videoconferencing, it is often impossible to "mix" or compose signals from different sources into a single split-screen image which is visible to everyone. In contrast, full-motion ITV provides signal-mixing capabilities, as in Figure 1, where we see a drawing displayed at one site sharing a split screen with students at another site. In the Hawai'i Interactive Television System (HITS), discussed in further detail in the following chapter, signals are sent from multiple sources — such as cameras at different sites, visual presenters (document cameras), computer displays, or video players — to a central control board where they are selected or "mixed" and re-transmitted as a "program" signal.

Figure 1. A drawing at one site shares a split screen with students at another site

In a videoconferencing environment unable to accommodate mixed programming, instructional strategies relying on mixing images on screen might have to be modified so that images are viewed alternately. This seemingly minor difference could have a noticeable effect on the success of a given activity.

The locus of technical control over the signal differs from system to system. In some systems, the teacher has access to a panel that may control robotic motion of cameras or switching between camera, visual presenter, and computer. In the HITS system, the teacher does not have a control panel; instead, a dedicated technician in a separate control room works in real time to select and mix incoming sources of input and place them on program. The technician decides what to place on program based on a combination of professional judgment and directions from the instructor which have been given in advance or are given in real time during transmission.

The implications of this difference between systems are twofold: instructors obliged to use the control panel will have to acquire the requisite technical skills, and instructors who must issue directions to a technician will have to deal with the extra time this requires. As technicians become more accustomed to an instructor's repertoire of activities, however, they may begin to anticipate needed camera angles, split screens, and so forth, so that they become active partners in instruction. In a sense, well-informed technicians such as these are "team teaching" with the instructor.

THE WORLD WIDE WEB

THE PRESENT

In terms of its advantages and disadvantages for distance education, the Web is very different from ITV, especially in the context of language instruction. Since the Web is evolving and means many things to many people, a current definition is probably in order: the World Wide Web consists of resources and users on the Internet utilizing HTTP (Hypertext Transfer Protocol), a set of rules for exchanging files, including text, graphic images, sound, video, and other multimedia (searchCRM.com, 2001).

Despite much talk about "virtual classrooms" on the Web, as of this writing the Web is unable to offer anything approaching ITV's replication of the face-to-face communicative environment of the traditional classroom. Despite advances in the handling of streaming media, at present it is still not practical for many learners to be brought together synchronously on the Web for classroom-type instruction including live audio and video such as is found on ITV. While streaming or archived media may be available to learners on the Web, it is unidirectional (from the instructor to the learner) and "canned" (i.e., prepackaged rather than composed in response to ongoing student needs), and students and instructors must rely on keyboarding for two-way communication.

THE FUTURE

Web technology advances quickly, and within the next few years it will become much easier for individual users (such as learners) to send and receive audio and video. Even when this happens, it cannot be assumed that the Web will be a popular medium for synchronous, or live, distance instruction. Due to the universal reach of the Web and the need in instructional contexts to archive submitted materials, it is more likely that teachers and learners will interact asynchronously by e-mailing video and/or audio "messages" to each other or placing them in discussion forums (also known as threaded discussions). Under these circumstances, strong initiative and autonomy will be required from each user as he or she records and posts to the forums; teacher support will be after-the-fact rather than ongoing in real time.

LANGUAGE INSTRUCTION

Given the current state of the World Wide Web and its probable direction of development, exclusively Web-delivered instruction is probably not appropriate for the beginning levels of language study. With little or no foundation in the language, beginning learners have special needs for instruction in the skills of listening and speaking. Ideally, they should receive ample ongoing, real-time support from a readily available instructor, and at present the Web is unable to facilitate such support. Instead, exclusively Web-based delivery is appropriate for skills other than speaking, and is especially suited to higher levels of language study where learners have established a foundation of reading and writing skills they can use independently as a means for two-way communication.

In contrast to ITV, Web-based technologies are relatively inexpensive, at least in terms of hardware. To the extent that students can be expected to provide their own means of access to the Web, capital expenses are limited to server and network hardware and software. There is no large-scale capital expense comparable to the construction of ITV studio classrooms at multiple sites, although human resources required for Web-based development, such as competitive salaries for good programmers, may be costly.

The portability of the Web means that it is suitable not only for *intercampus* delivery, but also for *interinstitutional* and *individual* delivery, that is, the offering of courses by one institution for another institution or for individuals from outside the institution.

Also unlike ITV, there is no need to consider limitations on the number of remote sites. However, this does not imply that an unlimited number of students may be served, since human factors still enter into determining the optimal size of the learning community and the ideal student/teacher ratio. For instance, given that one would expect an effective instructor to respond personally and fully to all the students online, the teacher's available time and energy would place a limit on the number of students one should have in a Web-based language class.

On the Web, the significance of geography is greatly reduced; learners may study at home, and, if the Web-based course is asynchronous, there is no requirement that all the students in a course log on at the same time. In fact, as long as the use of synchronous tools such as live chat (i.e., a messaging device allowing multiple users to gather in one or more virtual "rooms" to exchange messages in real time) is restricted to a few instances per semester, even students scattered across the globe may be persuaded to take part when synchronous activities are scheduled. So while the Web has certain limitations of application, it does offer global accessibility.

In the context of language instruction, it appears that Web-based distance education offers the strongest advantages for the teaching of languages in which learners with specialized needs for advanced instruction in skills other than speaking are widely scattered on the ground, even across institutional boundaries. This means that institutions with advanced instructional resources in less commonly taught languages can offer those resources to other institutions at which advanced instruction in those languages might otherwise not be available at all, as well as to individuals at widely scattered locations. For some less commonly taught languages, Web-based instruction may represent the only possibility for pulling together sufficient numbers of learners to make an advanced class viable at all. Given this potential for bringing widely scattered learners together at relatively low cost, Web technology will probably become a significant delivery medium for advanced language instruction in skills other than speaking in the near future.

DISTANCE EDUCATION AND DISTRIBUTED LEARNING

All education, not just distance education, has been revolutionized by the availability of electronic resources. The boundaries between distance education and traditional education are dissolving as both distance and non-distance classes make use of multiple technologies, especially the Web, for delivering educational resources — hence the term "distributed learning":

> Distributed learning is an instructional model that allows instructor, students, and content to be located in different, noncentralized locations so that instruction and learning occur independent of time and place. The distributed learning model can be used in combination with traditional classroom-based courses, with traditional distance learning courses, or it can be used to create wholly virtual classrooms (Saltzberg & Polyson, 1995, cited in Bowman, 1999).

Distributed learning models that combine different media to deliver instructional resources are increasingly common. Some of these are detailed below, with particular reference to language instruction.

ITV PLUS WEB-BASED DELIVERY

As noted above, ITV is a capital-intensive medium of instruction. At the same time, more disciplines are making use of ITV resources, and airtime is at a premium. Restricting ITV delivery to a few hours a week and "offloading" appropriate instructional activities to the Web allow an institution to economize on air time. In the language instruction context, during ITV airtime the focus is most logically placed on speaking and listening, while in the Web portion text-based activities, and possibly listening, can be highlighted. While such a model can help alleviate cost issues associated with ITV delivery, like ITV it falls short of providing global accessibility. Another liability of the "mixed delivery" model is its limited flexibility. Articulation from ITV to Web and back again on an almost daily basis requires strict adherence to a schedule, not to mention extremely meticulous planning and preparation — which must itself be factored as a cost.

OFFLINE OR INDEPENDENT LEARNING

Yet another element that may be introduced in a distributed learning "mix" is independent or "offline" learning. In this model of distributed learning, rather than delivering a steady stream of learning activities on an ongoing basis, the provider of instruction focuses on a process of preparing students for independent learning activities, and then following up on those activities. For instance, the following chapter presents a University of Hawai'i case study focusing on a Web-based course incorporating independent student use of a CD-ROM designed for self-instruction. After completing an initial sequence of activities at the course Web site, students use the CD-ROM offline, then return to the class Web site for follow-up and communicative tasks with classmates.

FURTHER DEVELOPMENTS IN DISTRIBUTED LEARNING

Distributed learning is becoming a point of convergence between traditional classroom instruction and distance education as more and more traditional classroom instructors offload portions of instructional activities to the Web. In some cases, Web-based activities, whether independent (such as reading assigned Web sites to obtain information) or group-based (such as threaded discussion), supplant classroom time. In this model, of course, learners do have F2F (face-to-face) time in the classroom, and so there is ample opportunity for treating listening and speaking skills in a communicative format. This "F2F advantage" is lacking in the strictly Web-based courses described above.

As models for distributed learning and distance education develop further, it is to be expected that the advantages of both Web-based instruction and F2F contact may be realized even in distance education situations by distributing the F2F portion of instruction among multiple tutors. In such a model, a Web-based course serves as a central point of contact between students and instructor who are separated by geographic distance. In the Web-based course, some activities are group-based, and some are independent, such as offline use of a CD-ROM. But in addition, as an integral part of the Web course, students are paired with a target language-speaking informant in their locale, recruited especially for the course and trained in a series of Web-based and telephone tutorials to engage in task-based speaking activities with small groups or individual students at specific points in the instructional sequence. The tutors are asked to engage in very specific tasks with the students and are directed to focus to the greatest extent possible on communication, rather than on language forms, during sessions with students. Students are directed to reserve questions about language forms (i.e., grammar and vocabulary) for the Web-based instructor. In this way, these questions and answers can be shared with all the students in a "grammar clinic" threaded discussion. Use of this model, combining the accessibility of distance education with the advantages of F2F contact, enables the Web to serve as the chief medium of language instruction even at beginning and intermediate levels, for which at present the Web alone is not sufficient.

PEER EDUCATION/DISTRIBUTED COGNITION

The definition of distributed learning provided earlier focuses on technological alternatives to the traditional classroom. In this definition, the word "distributed" refers to the distribution of instructional resources across multiple sites (such as ITV classrooms or individual computers) or modes of delivery (such as ITV plus Web). However, learning — especially language learning — has become more distributed in another sense as well in recent years. Advances in theories of learning based on social constructivism (Vygotsky, 1978) and distributed cognition (Pea, 1993, 1994; Salomon, 1993) have highlighted the importance of the background knowledge each learner brings to the learning process, the contributions each learner makes in the learning community, and the interplay between knowledge held in the mind and knowledge contained in artifacts such as learner notes and drafts, reference resources, and records of communicative interactions.

In the wake of these theoretical advances, instructional practices have moved away from teacher-centered models toward student-centered models featuring collaboration, communication, peer editing, and other practices which de-emphasize the teacher as sole bearer of authoritative or meaningful content and validate learners' ability to serve as educational resources for one another. For example, in the Web-based course which is the focus of the following chapter, the first activity in each unit is a "brainstorming" or information-sharing activity in which students contribute words, phrases, or facts that they already know to a class resource list accessible to everyone. Aside from fostering a sense of collaboration among students, this type of activity has the advantage of helping tailor instruction to the real needs of students as demonstrated by their current level of knowledge, rather than as anticipated by a teacher or textbook writer.

MAKING CHOICES FOR L2/FL DISTANCE EDUCATION

As indicated in the preceding sections, evolving definitions of distance education and of distributed learning point the way toward different choices for ITV-based, Web-based, and combined-delivery modes for second and foreign language instruction in different situations. Among the conclusions we can draw are

- Only *electronically-based* modes of delivery enabling *bi-directional communication* are appropriate for effective, communicative language instruction.
- Despite its relatively faithful reproduction of the communicative environment of the traditional classroom, ITV is expensive and limited in the area it can reach.
- ITV is appropriate for teaching beginning levels of less commonly taught languages within a single large, multi-campus institution, especially where student populations are too small to support instruction at a single location.

- Despite its relative economy, Web-based instruction does not (at present) adequately support instruction in speaking and, for this and other reasons, is not appropriate as an exclusive medium (i.e., without supplemental F2F instruction) for teaching beginning levels.

- Models of distributed learning for distance education combining Web-based and F2F components have the potential to strengthen the suitability of the Web as a medium for language instruction at the beginning and intermediate levels, since the F2F component is needed to support instruction in speaking.

- Web-based instruction is appropriate for advanced instruction of students with specialized needs for language development and maintenance in skills other than speaking. In some cases, the gathering together of learners across institutional boundaries to form a Web-based "learning community" may represent the only viable alternative for advanced instruction in a given language.

- With adequate planning and preparation — and careful adherence to a schedule — Web-based and ITV instruction can be combined in appropriate ways to reduce ITV air time and associated expenses.

- Independent, or "offline," learning can be used to advantage in distributed learning models for advanced language instruction. Models featuring independent learning must pay particular attention to preparation for independent work and to follow-up activities.

- Student-centered activities are an important element in modern models for language instruction and add a new dimension to the definition of "distributed learning."

WHERE DO WE GO FROM HERE?

With the advent of the Information Age, distance-delivered education has grown exponentially in a few short years and will continue to grow in the foreseeable future. What is the future of distance-delivered language education? Distance-delivered language education may evolve, or it may decline in a backlash if online learners find that what was promised has not been delivered. Teaching performance-based subjects, such as languages, presents a special challenge for distance educators and distance learners because technology in 2002 does not yet adequately support four-skill language instruction online. Where do we go from here?

Beginning students today cannot learn to speak, listen, read, and write a language effectively when the sole medium of delivery is online instruction. Therefore distributed learning is likely to evolve creatively and with varying degrees of success until online learning can reliably support and deliver multi-modality interaction to a mass audience. Distributed learning, an approach that allows instructor, students, and content to be situated in different locations and instruction and learning to occur independent of time and place and via multiple mediums of instruction, is likely to be central to any successful distance-delivered language instruction in the immediate future.

REFERENCES

Bowman, M. (1999). What is distributed learning? *Tech Sheet, 2*(1). Retrieved February 19, 2001, from:
http://techcollab.monterey.edu/techsheet2.1/distributed.html

Keegan, D. (1990). *Foundations of distance education* (2nd ed.). London: Routledge.

Omaggio Hadley, A. (2001). *Teaching language in context* (3rd ed.). Boston: Heinle & Heinle.

Pea, R. D. (1993). Practices of distributed intelligence and designs for education. In G. Salomon (Ed.), *Distributed Cognitions* (pp. 47–87). Cambridge, England: Cambridge University Press.

Pea, R. D. (1994). Seeing what we build together: Distributed multimedia learning environments for transformative communications. *The Journal of the Learning Sciences, 3*(3), 285–299.

Saettler, P. (1990). *The evolution of American educational technology.* Englewood, CO: Libraries Unlimited.

Salomon, G. (1993). No distribution without individual's cognition: a dynamic interactional view. In G. Salomon (Ed.), *Distributed Cognitions* (pp. 111–138). Cambridge, England: Cambridge University Press.

Saltzberg, S., & Polyson, S. (1995). Distributed learning on the World Wide Web. *Syllabus, 9*(1). [text file]. Retrieved February 19, 2001, from:
http://www.syllabus.com/archive/Syll95/07_sept95/DistrLrngWWWeb.txt

SearchCRM.com. Retrieved September 5, 2001, from:
http://searchcrm.techtarget.com/sDefinition/0,,sid11_gci213391,00.html

Vygotsky, L. S. (1978). *Mind in society: the development of higher psychological processes.* Cambridge, MA: Harvard University Press.

Stephen Fleming, David Hiple, & Yun Du
University of Hawai'i at Mānoa

FOREIGN LANGUAGE DISTANCE EDUCATION: THE UNIVERSITY OF HAWAI'I EXPERIENCE

The overriding rationale for distance education is accessibility: making opportunities for learning available to those who would otherwise not have such opportunities. The College of Languages, Linguistics and Literature at the University of Hawai'i at Mānoa has undertaken research and development initiatives and become a leader in distance-delivered language education because practical necessity has required it. Hawai'i is the most isolated state in the United States, and its island geography makes its citizens isolated not only from the mainland but from one another.

What is the responsibility of the University of Hawai'i at Mānoa in urban Honolulu on O'ahu to answer the request of the student at Maui Community College who wants to study Chinese even though it is not offered on her campus? What is the responsibility of the University of Hawai'i to answer the request of the businessman in St. Louis who wants to undertake language study in preparation for a work assignment in Seoul? What is the responsibility of the University of Hawai'i to answer the request of the students at a small liberal arts college in Iowa who have studied two years of Japanese but cannot continue because there is not a cohort on their campus large enough to justify a third year course?

In the United States, language education is increasingly divided into the "commonly taught languages" and the "less commonly taught languages" (LCTLs). Spanish is commonly taught; Korean is less commonly taught; Filipino, Samoan, and Vietnamese are much less commonly taught. Yet in Hawai'i, Japanese is the most commonly taught language, and at the University of Hawai'i it is possible to study a four-year sequence of Chinese, Filipino, Hawaiian, Ilokano, Japanese, Korean, Samoan, or Vietnamese, as well as French, German, Russian, or Spanish. Ideally, learners throughout the United States should be able to study LCTLs offered at UH which are not offered in their own locality.

In an attempt to meet the needs and fulfill the desires of heritage students, isolated "nontraditional" learners, and small educational institutions offering lower division language programs only, the University of Hawai'i sought support from the National Security Education Program (NSEP) to embark on a plan to deliver less commonly taught languages via distance education. This case study is a report on Hawai'i's efforts to develop models for delivery of critical languages via distance education.

Fleming, S., Hiple, D., & Du, Y. (2002). Foreign language distance education: The University of Hawai'i experience. In C. A. Spreen (Ed.), *New technologies and language learning: Cases in the less commonly taught languages* (Technical Report #25; pp. 13–54). Honolulu, HI: University of Hawai'i, Second Language Teaching & Curriculum Center.

The University of Hawai'i has received two grants from NSEP to carry out distance education projects in critical languages. The first was a two-year grant conducted 1995–1997 to develop a model a) to facilitate the broad-based teaching and learning of LCTLs via interactive television (ITV) so as to reach underaccommodated regions and populations and to increase U.S. capacity in critical languages, b) to create a 2-year (four semester) distance-education course sequence in Mandarin Chinese and to field test and deliver the course over ITV with integrated Internet formats, and c) to disseminate electronically a teachers' manual modeling current pedagogy for teaching via the medium of ITV.

The second two-year grant, conducted 1999–2002, again focused on development and dissemination of distance education models. In the area of dissemination, a series of workshops was conducted nationwide to teach faculty to use to their advantage interactive television and integrated formats in distance-delivered, performance-based language teaching. Since most ITV language instruction takes place across multi-campus public institutions, the workshops were conducted via the ITV medium itself to faculty participating at multiple sites within the same systems.

The development component of the second NSEP grant focused on creating and teaching World Wide Web (WWW)-delivered upper division Chinese and Korean language courses. The model featured advanced, third-year reading-writing and listening-reading-writing courses utilizing CD-ROMs developed at the University of Hawai'i and featuring authentic source material and activities.

At all stages of the course, the teacher was actively involved with the students via a Web forum, which facilitated the carrying out of daily tasks and team assignments. The teacher managed and monitored student progress and gave feedback through numerous lesson phases, including a Grammar Clinic where selected student postings were identified and "workshopped" by the class. A language exchange near the end of the term also featured Web-based exchange with native speakers in Taiwan or Korea. Student feedback was elicited via anonymous Web-based questionnaires at various points during the course.

As has been stated, the two UH NSEP grants were carried out to meet the immediate needs and fulfill the desires of heritage students, isolated "nontraditional" learners, and small educational institutions lacking upper division courses. Additionally, however, the University of Hawai'i, through its NSEP grants, also sought to undertake research in two increasingly interrelated areas: a) learning theory within the context of technology-delivered distance education, and b) approaches to language pedagogy within the context of technology-delivered distance education.

Constructivist learning theory postulates that learning is the process of constructing knowledge from experiences (Driscoll, 1994); social constructivists believe knowledge is accumulated by learners through social interaction (Vygotsky, 1978). Therefore, the process of knowledge construction depends not only on the individual learner but on the interactive environment. What are the implications of Vygotskian learning theory on constructing and coordinating Web-based courses and nurturing online language learning communities?

Most Web-delivered courses tend to be content-based. For example, a history course focuses on mastery of material relating to events in a specific time period. It is not difficult to imagine a Web-based history course featuring off-line readings and some online dialogue culminating in a research paper. But what of the Web-delivered, performance-based language course? How does the instructor teach students to read and write in Chinese on line?

This case study will provide a brief report on Hawai'i's ITV methodology workshops and Web-based courses, and research findings focusing on instruments and procedures for evaluating Web-based learning environments, Web-based learning experiences, and Web-based learning outcomes.

THE UH APPROACH

The University of Hawai'i began its distance education initiatives in 1995 as part of an effort to establish models for bringing instructional resources in less commonly taught languages to widely dispersed, underserved populations of learners. To this end, under two separate grant initiatives funded by the National Security Education Program, project teams from the Second Language Teaching and Curriculum Center of the College of Languages, Linguistics and Literature worked over several years to devise, test, and disseminate strategies for the design and delivery of foreign language instruction via distance education media. The principal goal of the first project was to develop and deliver beginning and intermediate level instruction via ITV; the goal of the second project was to develop and deliver instruction at the advanced level via the Web.

In this chapter a description of the ITV and Web courses will be followed by a more detailed examination of outcomes in one Web-based course.

ITV COURSES

The primary motivation for offering language education at a distance is to reach populations of learners to whom instruction in the language would otherwise be unavailable. Among the various options for delivery of distance education, ITV most closely replicates the environment of the traditional bricks-and-mortar classroom. Two-way audio and video enable learners to participate in listening and speaking activities that would be impossible to replicate in other distance-education media, such as the Web. Since listening and speaking skills are particularly important at beginning levels of instruction, ITV is very suitable for delivery of beginning and intermediate language instruction. This is why ITV was chosen in this distance education project as the medium for delivery of first- and (subsequently) second-year Chinese language instruction to students at multiple

UH system campuses throughout the Island State where postsecondary Chinese language instruction would otherwise be unavailable.

The University of Hawai'i system, which includes all the state's community colleges as well as its three four-year campuses, is fortunate to possess an outstanding interactive television system which was created by an act of the legislature of the State of Hawai'i in 1984 and fully deployed in 1990. The infrastructure of the Hawai'i Interactive Television System, or HITS, enables full-motion two-way video to be carried via point-to-point microwave transmission between multiple locations throughout the Islands. As part of the University's Information Technology Services (ITS) division, HITS makes its technology and personnel available for the delivery of instructional programs to parts of the state where they would otherwise be unavailable. Most of these programs originate at UH Mānoa in Honolulu, the flagship campus of the UH system, and can include up to four additional remote classroom sites participating via two-way video. The existence of HITS made Hawai'i an excellent proving ground for the development of instructional models for foreign language via ITV. Prior to this project, courses in foreign language had never been offered over HITS. The focus of the project was to discover ways to implement task-based, communicative language learning activities in the ITV context.

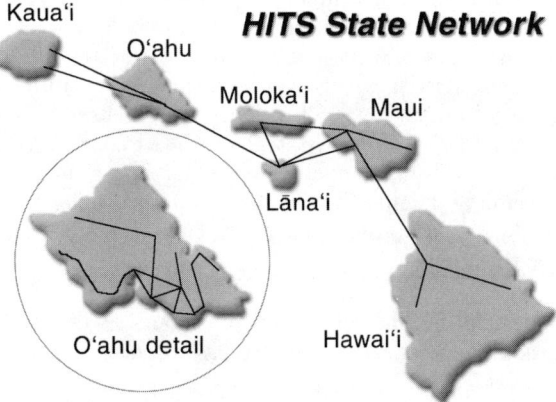

Figure 1. Schematic representation of the Hawai'i Interactive Television System network

The first Chinese ITV course, CHN 101, was launched in Fall 1995, with a complement of 11 students at Mānoa and 15 students distributed across four remote sites on three islands. Students who enrolled at these "remote sites" included those who were interested in Chinese language for reasons connected with their profession (such as a doctor of Chinese traditional medicine), those who were interested in traveling to China, and community college students who wished to complete the foreign language study requirement for their BA degree before transferring to a four-year campus. Over the next 2 academic years, the course sequence was expanded to cover a full two-year sequence, with first- and second-year courses running simultaneously. Several of the students from the original CHN 101 cohort continued taking HITS Chinese classes for the full two-year sequence.

Administrative preparations and provisions: Meeting the challenges

ITV-based foreign language education is presented with considerable administrative complications as it reaches across campus-to-campus — and even institution-to-institution — boundaries to bring together scattered populations of learners. Registration procedures, tuition rates, and publicity all pose challenges that must be resolved in order for ITV courses to be offered successfully. As a result of this project, much knowledge was gained about administrative aspects of offering courses over ITV. Much of this knowledge came to light during the instructional planning phase.

Registration of students from multiple campuses was facilitated by an existing systemwide arrangement under which registrars at the various campuses of the University of Hawai'i system processed registrations on behalf of the originating campus. Academic credit is automatically and directly transferable from one campus in the University of Hawai'i system to another, so issues of credit transfer did not arise. However, there was no unified system for *publicizing* HITS courses across all campuses, and publicity varied in scope and quality. Recruiting students was difficult in locales where publicity was weak. Given the UH experience, foreign language distance educators planning courses would be well advised to pay close attention to publicity and the facilitation of cross-campus recruitment and registration.

Tuition discrepancies were the major point of difference between campuses that caused headaches for the course developers. Courses offered on HITS are "housed" at one school, usually the campus of the University of Hawai'i system from which the program originates. This most often is UH Mānoa. Most courses on HITS are part of professional degree programs such as nursing or business, and registration for the courses is only possible by matriculating in the program, which is offered by UH Mānoa. Tuition for these courses is charged at the four-year campus rate, which is considerably higher than at the two-year community college campuses. The lower-division Chinese courses did not fit into this "professional training" model. University of Hawai'i system community college students who are not in professional training programs expect to pay community college tuition for lower-division courses, which they often subsequently transfer to a four-year campus when they matriculate there. If offered at the four-year-campus tuition rate, the Chinese courses were not competitively priced and were too expensive for community college students.

It became clear that no matter what solution was adopted, cross-campus differences in tuition were always going to be difficult to resolve. In the end, in order to attract students at multiple campuses, the course was offered under a special arrangement free of charge to students at remote sites (i.e., at the community colleges). This tuition waiver was possible only with the support of external funding from NSEP. In the second year, this arrangement was modified by cross-listing the course at a community college and at the four-year campus, thus enabling students to register for the course through the community college, paying the lower rate. But this resulted in reduced tuition revenue for UH Mānoa, the originating campus. If the instructor's salary had not been supported by external funding, the course could not have been offered. All of these arrangements required considerable time and effort on our part as well as the cooperation of support staff in many locations. Tuition differences across campuses and the ability of the targeted student population to pay, as well as the balance between tuition revenue and instructor compensation, will be important considerations for institutions planning to offer ITV-based language courses.

Another issue in offering the courses across campuses was reconciling academic schedules. While the academic calendar was the same, class times during the day differed from campus to campus. HITS programming slots were only available at the top of the hour, while on most campuses classes began at half past the hour. For many students, the 50-minute class stretched across two class periods on their campus, creating conflicts which reduced the courses' attractiveness. In the end, only students who could tolerate the conflict enrolled. Although it seems a small detail, the issue of class times and academic calendars can pose major challenges for institutions offering courses via ITV.

Instructional strategies for ITV delivery of foreign language instruction

ITV is a special educational medium requiring adaptation of instructional strategies — namely, adaptations in classroom organization, student grouping, and in content or document delivery. As mentioned in chapter 1, among all the different distance education media — including Web-based instruction, one-way TV, and others — ITV is the medium that comes closest to recreating the traditional classroom setting. Nevertheless, there are great differences between the ITV classroom and the traditional classroom, as the following discussion will illustrate.

Classroom organization

Well-trained language teachers know the importance of managing classroom space and time through careful organization of seating arrangements, teacher position in the classroom, activity duration, and so forth (see, e.g., Gower, Philips. & Walters, 1995). In the unique environment of the ITV classroom, assumptions that are taken for granted in the ordinary classroom, such as relative freedom of movement or easy audibility, no longer hold. Students and teacher are placed into an audially and visually fragmented environment in which speaking to one's classmates or forming groups for a communicative activity requires deliberate effort. In this environment, classroom activities must be adapted from their usual forms if they are to work at all, and both students and teacher must learn new ways of participating in the classroom community.

An ITV class is conducted simultaneously at multiple locations: the originating site, where the teacher is located; and one or more remote sites. These sites are connected by video lines. Several cameras at the originating site are available to capture the image of the instructor and/or the students there. Each remote site has, in general, only one camera, which captures the image of the students at that site.

As shown in Figure 2, each remote site is connected separately to the originating site, where the video signals coming in are

- displayed on television monitors along the back wall of the classroom, so that the instructor can see all sites at all times; and
- made available to the engineers as potential material for display on the "program" signal, alone or in combination with other images. (Figure 3 shows the mixing board where incoming signals are mixed and sent out again "on program.")

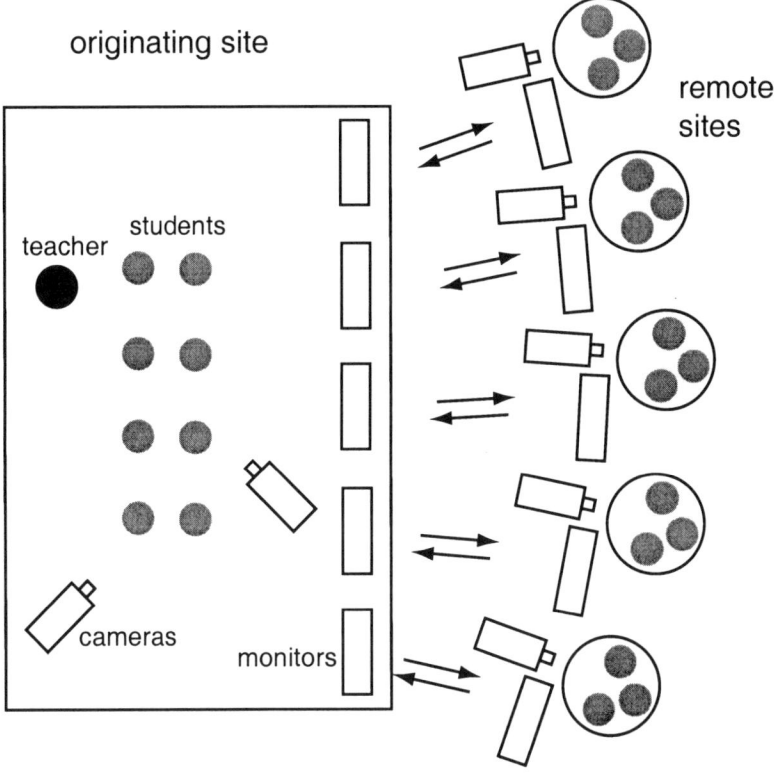

Figure 2. Schematic of originating classroom and remote-site classrooms

The "program" signal is sent out to all sites, where it appears on the television monitor at each site (including the originating site, where it is visible on at least one monitor). Since the "program" signal is the only signal received at the remote sites, students at those sites only see what is placed "on program." They do not see the entire class at all sites in the same way the instructor at the originating classroom does. The instructor must take care when conducting activities to make sure that all relevant visuals are visible on program.

Figure 3. Control room: Images from various sources are available for placement "on program"

The teacher in the ITV classroom sits at a special "station" at the originating site which consists of a chair and table plus special technical equipment, and faces the class (see Figure 4). This furniture configuration is similar to that in the traditional classroom except for the presence of the additional equipment. The presence of the equipment and the necessity of avoiding sudden moves out of camera range limit the instructor's mobility and create a certain amount of separation from the students, even at the originating site. The sense of separation between teacher and students, and between student and student, can be even more pronounced at remote sites, where students generally sit in rows facing a camera and a monitor. With no live teacher in the remote-site classroom, the spatial environment is centered more around the television monitor, while in the originating classroom, the students have to decide whether to watch the "real" teacher or the teacher on the television monitors. With planning and experience, the sense of physical and psychological separation engendered by the technology can be mitigated through use of the technology to create interaction and a sense of community on program, equalizing the remote sites' and the originating site's sense of participation and access. Pair- and group-work, or the adaptations of pair- and group-work described below, are especially useful in creating this sense of community, since they tend to engage the student as a communicator rather than as a mere spectator.

Figure 4. Teacher and students at originating classroom; Remote sites are visible on monitors at the back of the room

As the first UH Chinese course began on HITS, time was required for both teacher and students to adjust to this unfamiliar medium. Training for ITV instructors and students was provided by HITS support staff, covering on-camera behavior such as verbal self-identification, use of the visual presenter (also known as a document camera or ELMO®), and use of the microphones. This training, while helpful, was not geared to the special needs of communicative language instruction, and it soon became plain that the generic teaching and learning behaviors reflected in the training were suitable only some of the time in the language classroom. The ITV medium is naturally suited to a "talking head" style of presentation — that is, teacher-fronted lectures with intermittent display of visual media. But current language teaching practice has removed teacher-fronted activities from the central role and instead emphasizes communicative use of language in naturalistic situations, with a special focus on communicative tasks. Therefore special efforts were needed to adapt language teaching activities for use in the ITV environment.

Student grouping

In the communicative language classroom many classroom activities typically involve pairwork (including serial pairwork or "mingling") and small group work. The ITV medium poses challenges for implementing these activities. As the Chinese ITV course continued over several semesters, a set of strategies for adapting such activities was developed. These adaptive strategies can be roughly divided into two large types. Adaptations of the first type are aimed at reducing or replacing simultaneous channels of communication — in other words, changing the management of activities in which many different people are speaking at the same time. This type of adaptation is necessary because on ITV only one communication channel is available at any one time between sites. The second type of adaptive strategies involves finding effective methods or substitutions for document delivery — in other words, finding ways to deal with the need to distribute visuals (e.g., student drawings), worksheets, and other documents at short notice, even when students are divided across multiple sites. These two basic types of adaptations require careful attention to student grouping, use of the single communicative channel, and use of the images placed "on program" for everyone to see. These adaptations are discussed below.

Instructional strategies pair- and group-work. In the communicatively oriented language classroom, activities in which students work together as pairs or groups occupy significant portions of class time. In such activities, multiple conversations are carried on simultaneously. Part of the reason for limiting the number of students in language skill classes is to enable pairs and groups to form and re-form easily and to enable the instructor to actively monitor group performance. While the design and management of pair- and group-work becomes second nature for instructors in the traditional classroom, those new to ITV may be unaware of the very different conditions in the traditional classroom and the ITV classroom. This lack of awareness can make managing pair- and group-work activities difficult on ITV.

In the traditional classroom, pairs or groups are distributed around the room. All conversations are carried on the same air, and the hubbub may be such that the instructor, doubtless happy that the activity has excited the students, must nevertheless intervene and appeal for everyone to speak more quietly. Even when the noise is considerable, however, pairs or groups sitting together have no problem focusing on one another's utterances. As long as one is face to face with a conversational partner, it is possible to filter out a considerable amount of background noise. During the activity, the instructor can circulate freely in the room to deal with questions and to monitor individual pairs and groups, perhaps "harvesting" examples of student utterances to deal with afterwards. And when the activity is finished, it is usually not too difficult for the instructor to get everyone's attention. At this point, groups and pairs may be rapidly reconfigured for an extension of the activity.

In the ITV environment, many seemingly commonsense assumptions about what is possible in an activity are turned on their head. The usually singular, unified classroom environment is fragmented. Assuming that students are present in the originating classroom, the instructor is physically present only for these students. The remote-site classrooms see the instructor only on screen. While communication among students at each site is carried through the classroom air at that site (as in the traditional classroom), conversations *across* sites — including anything the instructor wants to say to everyone — must be carried over the audio channel. In ordinary F2F (face-to-face) conversation, people speaking to one another can understand one another even if there is background noise, such as other conversations nearby. Non-verbal cues such as facial expressions help carry the message, and it is easy to focus on the other person. But speech carried over ITV audio, somewhat like speech over the telephone, is usually only intelligible if there is little background noise AND only one utterance is being carried over the channel. This means that in any site-to-site communication, only one person may speak at a time; everyone else must listen, or at least not disturb the conversation. At the same time, background noise is more complicated than in the traditional classroom: Each site has its own "hubbub," which, depending on whether microphones are on or off, may or may not be audible to the other sites. Instructor announcements over the audio channel may go unnoticed if a site is involved in its own hubbub, or if other noise is coming through active microphones. In effect, the instructor is externalized from the remote-site classrooms, and must adapt special strategies to manage remote-site classrooms "through the screen."

The physical isolation of one site from the next means that options are limited for reconfiguring pairs and groups for continuation or extension of an activity: At a given site, only so many combinations will be possible. If total enrollment at all sites has been limited to a number corresponding to the usual number in a traditional language classroom, some sites may have very few students, or even a single student who can only be paired or grouped with students at other sites.

While the instructor can manage activities at the originating site in a fashion similar to that in the traditional classroom, adaptive strategies are needed to manage activities at the remote sites and to manage interaction among all the sites. Some general strategies are

- to use a language comprehensible to the technician to issue verbal instructions for the performance of an activity and for technical requirements connected with it, such as certain camera shots;
- to designate specific sites and specific students in one's spoken instructions, so that both students and technicians know how the channel is going to be used;
- to specify clearly which microphones should be on, and which off, during the activity;
- to issue instructions for configuring (and re-configuring) groups in advance — in other words, to assign partners for one or more iterations of an activity so that no break will be needed to re-group students;
- to set time limits in advance, so that at a pre-arranged signal the activity will shift gears or come to an end;
- to designate a concrete "product" for each communicative activity, for instance a worksheet on which prices must be filled in for at least 10 items based on information received;
- if possible, to model the activity with a student or group of students at the origination site prior to beginning the activity itself (see Figure 5).

If pairs or groups can successfully be formed at each site, then the channel does not need to be used for communication during the activity. In this case, prompts or supporting materials (such as sentence patterns) may be placed on program using the visual presenter or a computer screen, and students can proceed with the activity separately at the various sites. Since the channel is not being used for communication, all microphones are turned off. But in case the teacher wishes to monitor what is happening at a remote site, he may request microphones to be turned on at that site while he listens in with headphones. (The loudspeakers in all classrooms are turned down, so the material coming through the active microphone does not disturb other students.)

Figure 5. Activity modeling: teacher and student at originating classroom try activity first while everyone else listens

Alternative instructional strategies — public and private channels. If pairs or groups cannot be formed "evenly" within each site — for example, if there is a single student at any site — then alternative arrangements must be made. There are two major strategies to approach this problem:

- *"Private channel" strategy.* Assign one pair or group to interact on program using microphones and (possibly) headphones while everyone else works "traditional-style" (off-program) and ignores the group on program;

- *"Public forum" strategy.* Substitute a whole-class activity for the pair- or group-work activity, with everyone participating on-program.

If the "private channel" strategy is selected, all students other than those in the on-program pair or group must be in a pair or group at their own site. The group of students communicating on program should be no larger than three or four, but additional students may be assigned a "receptive" or listening role in the activity. Measures must be taken to visually and aurally separate the students on program from other students at their respective sites. This is accomplished as follows:

- If possible, all students on the "private channel" should be visible on screen through the use of split-screen technology. For example, in Figure 6, one student has been placed in an inset.

- At any site where "private channel" users and non-users are together in the same classroom, they should, if possible, be aurally isolated from one another. One practical solution is to have the "private channel" user(s) wear headphones, while the loudspeakers on the television monitors are muted. It is helpful to have an additional pair of headphones available at the originating site so that the teacher can listen in on the "private channel" users periodically.

Figure 6. One pair uses the channel privately. One student is alone at her remote site; the other uses headphones to block "hubbub" at her own site.

While the "private channel" strategy may seem elaborate, after a few attempts it tends to run more smoothly as it becomes part of the classroom culture for students, the instructor, and the technicians. In the follow-up phase of the activity, when the instructor has drawn everyone's attention back together to "see how things went," the results from the "private channel" pair or group can simply be integrated with the results from other pairs or groups in the checking process.

The "public forum" strategy may take a number of forms, but its basic intent is to consolidate many pairs or groups into one large group — the entire class — while still giving every student a chance to speak. A typical adaptation is to take so-called "serial pairwork" activity and change it into a panel discussion. A serial pairwork activity, as realized in the traditional classroom, is one in which students interact briefly with a series of partners to get one piece of information from each. A typical serial pairwork activity, "Who Drew This?", is described below, followed by a description of its adaptation.

- In preparation for the traditional classroom version of this activity, each student is asked to create a visual representation of something he is going to talk about. For example, if the task is to find out facts about where someone went on vacation and what kind of transport he used to get to each destination, students are directed to draw a map of their trip with destinations numbered and icons of trains, planes, and so forth between the destinations. The drawings are not to be labeled with the artist's name.

- Before the instructor gathers the drawings, he directs the students to make sure they will be able to answer questions about the places they went and how they got there. Then he gathers the drawings and either displays them all in a central location or redistributes them so that each student receives a drawing he did not make.

- Students interview one another about their trips with the objective of identifying the author of each drawing. If all drawings are centrally located, then after interviewing one partner, a student can point to the correct drawing, and then move on to the next partner. If each student has received a drawing, he interviews partners until he finds the person who made the drawing he has received.

In the ITV classroom it is not possible for students to rotate through partners at multiple sites, so a "public forum" adaptation of this activity may be performed, as follows:

- Once students have made their drawings, the teacher chooses one. If the chosen drawing is from the origination site, the teacher keeps track of who drew it, and without revealing that person's identity displays the drawing on the visual presenter. Alternatively, the teacher may request that one of the drawings at a remote site where there are at least three students be placed on the visual presenter there. (In this case, the teacher may not know who made the drawing.)
- Without revealing specifically who made the drawing, the teacher directs the camera to show three people sitting in a row, one of whom is the author of the drawing. The image of this "panel" is placed on program along with the drawing via split screen technology (See Figure 7).
- Opening a "public forum," the teacher directs all members of the class to ask questions of the panel members about their destinations and how they got to each. Each student must ask one question, which may be a repetition of an earlier question.
- After the round of questioning, the class is asked to identify the author of the drawing.

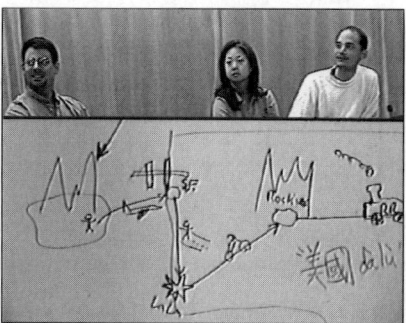

Figure 7. "Public forum" adaptation. The panel members (at top) are interviewed about their respective journeys to see whose description matches the travel map.

In using the adaptations described above, the teacher's approach to giving students feedback need not change. Generally speaking, the approach favored in current pedagogy is to allow communication to proceed uninterrupted unless students request help; erroneous utterances heard during communication can be brought into focus at the end of the activity.

The "private channel" and "public forum" adaptations cover a lot of situations, but may not suffice for every eventuality. Creative instructors must experiment until they find adaptations that work in their particular situations.

New strategies for document delivery and display

As mentioned above, aside from strategies for student grouping, the other large category of adaptive strategies for ITV-based foreign language instruction centers around finding effective methods or substitutions for document delivery — in other words, finding ways to deal with the need to distribute drawings or worksheets at short notice, even when students are divided across multiple sites.

In the communicatively oriented language classroom, many activities require students to work with visual artifacts and documents, such as drawings and written descriptions. In such activities, a visual and its corresponding written description may be separated and distributed at random to students; the student task is to match up each description with its corresponding visual by reading and understanding the description.

This theme of matching visual to text can be extended to listening and speaking; creation of the drawing or artifact may be woven into the activity itself, as when a student draws a representation of what his partner is saying. The common thread among the variants is that they all require redistribution of drawings and documents among students. In the traditional classroom, this is a simple matter of gathering up the pieces and passing them out again, or posting drawings on a bulletin board. In the ITV environment, documents can be distributed by the alternative means of mail, fax, and visual presenter. Choosing the appropriate alternative in each instance of requires consideration of a number of factors.

Worksheets, tests, or visuals that the instructor can prepare well in advance of a certain date can be duplicated and mailed to arrive in time to be distributed by on-site staff. Naturally, this means of distribution is preferred by ITV support staff, since it is most convenient for them. As mentioned above, however, modern language pedagogy stresses the importance of student-centered, communicative activities, and much of the time these require the use of student-produced writings and drawings. Because mailing requires a long lead-time, it is not a good means for distributing student-produced content. In most cases, instruction moves too quickly for regular mail to be useful as a means for students to exchange writings or visuals based on a current lesson.

Fax transmission can serve as an alternative for document delivery, but faxing has its limitations, and so it cannot serve as a simple substitute for passing documents by hand. Any document that is transmitted by fax must be handled on the far end by ITV support staff, whether receiving or sending. Clear instructions must be provided with documents faxed to remote sites as to whether the documents must be copied and distributed, distributed individually, or handled by some other arrangement. Fax transmission is suitable for black and white line drawings, but not for color or high-resolution items. Items written or drawn in pencil do not transmit well.

The visual presenter enables display of documents, visuals, or small objects in full color. Text documents in letters smaller than 36 points or so usually cannot be displayed in their entirety; for smaller text to be read, a portion of the document is viewed in a zoom (close) shot.

Adapting an activity for the ITV classroom

The following is a practical example of the adaptation of an activity for the traditional classroom for use in the ITV instructional format. The activity is communicative and task-based; in other words, information flows from one student to another via the target language (in this case, a written text), and the information is used to accomplish a purpose (the matching of a text with a drawing or other graphic). The various steps that must be taken to implement the activity are outlined in detail.

Reading/writing activity "Who wrote this?"

In the traditional classroom version of "Who wrote this?" each student creates a "visual" (a drawing or graphic) and a matching text on the topic of the assignment — for example, a picture of a yard and a house with a corresponding written description. The visuals and the texts are gathered by the teacher and any names are erased. The visuals are displayed at a central location (such as a bulletin board); the texts are redistributed. In the reading portion of the activity, students read the text they have been given and attempt to match it to its corresponding visual, relying only on information in the text. Students may trade texts for a reiteration of the activity.

A close replication of the traditional classroom version of "Who wrote this?" is impossible, or at least impractical, in the ITV classroom. Simultaneous display of all visuals (as on the bulletin board) is impossible in the ITV medium. Only one, or perhaps two, visuals may be displayed at once on the visual presenter. Redistribution of all visuals and texts would involve two series of faxes: first, remote-site students would have to fax visuals and texts to the originating site, and then the originating site would have to fax visuals and texts for individual redistribution to the remote sites — an extremely cumbersome and time-consuming proposition.

There are two basic approaches for adapting the "Who wrote this?" activity for the ITV classroom. Both involve selective use of the fax and visual presenter.

Alternative 1. Before class, remote-site students fax their writings to the instructor. The instructor chooses three writings from any three students (originating site or remote site) and copies them, or cuts-and-pastes them, onto a single page, which is then faxed to the remote sites. In the best case, copies of this fax are made on the spot for each remote-site student. The same sheet may be copied for the originating-site students, or they may receive randomly distributed writings by their classmates. The instructor first asks students to read the writings they have received, singly or in pairs or groups, and to predict the appearance of the drawings that would correspond to the readings. The instructor then uses the visual presenter to display drawings from the origination site sequentially, and asks students at the remote sites to use their visual presenters to do the same.

Each time students perform a positive identification between the drawing on display and the writing they are looking at, they are asked to call out. At this point, they may be asked to read aloud so that others can confirm their ID. This adaptation may be seen in Figure 8.

Alternative 2. If faxing is not possible, a whole-class version of the activity may be implemented using the visual presenter exclusively. The instructor gathers writings and drawings from the originating-site students. The instructor displays one drawing and asks students to work in pairs to predict what they will see in the corresponding writing. The instructor then displays writings sequentially for students to read, and asks students to call out when the writing that matches the drawing appears.

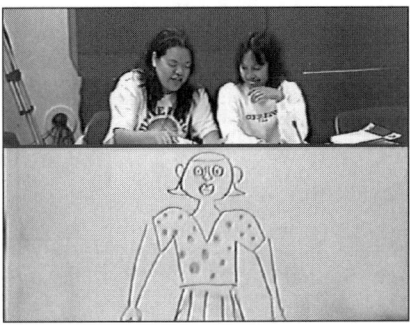

Figure 8. Students placed into a split screen read aloud a student-produced text they have received to confirm that it matches the student-produced visual the teacher has displayed on the visual presenter.

The Hawai'i ITV experience

The project team found that despite its vast differences with the traditional classroom, ITV is a viable medium of instruction for all the skills that are taught in the bricks-and-mortar foreign language classroom, as long as careful consideration is given to the adaptation of communicative activities to suit the demands of the ITV environment. During several years of experience with Chinese language instruction via ITV, the project team observed the following:

- Student reaction to the courses, as indicated in end-of-semester evaluations and day-to-day interactions, was favorable. Students with no other alternatives for taking Chinese were particularly appreciative of the courses.

- Student participation in the classroom community, despite the constraints imposed by the medium, was active and social, especially during communicative activities, according to teachers' reported experience. Despite geographical separation, students at different sites got to know each other during the classes, forming a single, cohesive classroom community.

- Student achievement was comparable to that in the traditional classroom, despite the extra time needed to deal with the special demands of the ITV medium: setting up activities, communicating with technical personnel, sending and receiving faxes, and a greater proportion of "are you there?"–type phatic communication than in ordinary classroom discourse.

- Students were successfully streamed into other courses, or experienced communicative success when traveling in the target language environment (China and Taiwan).

- Access to Chinese language instruction at the postsecondary beginning level was broadened statewide.

- ITV proved a robust medium for the delivery of communicative language instruction at the beginning and intermediate levels in all four skills.

In order to share our experience with foreign language instructors using ITV at other institutions in the United States, the project team developed Web-based and workshop resources. The following tasks were completed as a dissemination component of this project:

- "Best practices" for foreign language instruction via ITV were disseminated nationwide via a summer institute and accompanying videoconference, as well as three well-received workshops, each serving multiple locations via ITV, at state universities in California, New York, and Wisconsin.

- A Web site, http://nflrc.hawaii.edu/sfleming/flitv, was developed and published to serve as a resource for ITV-based foreign language instructors.

WEB-BASED COURSES

As mentioned in chapter 1, ITV represents the most appropriate choice for beginning and intermediate language classes. Current language pedagogy stresses the importance of all four skills in the early stages of language training. ITV is currently the only distance technology that offers a communicative environment comparable to a bricks-and-mortar classroom, and therefore only ITV can provide a distance environment adequate for training in the skills of listening and speaking.

Although exclusively Web-delivered instruction is probably not appropriate for teaching four-skills courses at the beginning or intermediate levels of language study, Web-based delivery *is* appropriate for skills other than speaking, and is especially suited to higher levels of language study where learners have established a foundation of reading and writing skills they can use independently as a means for two-way communication. The universal reach of the Web extends accessibility to these courses far beyond the reach of ITV courses, offering learning opportunities both for students at institutions not offering advanced training and for mid-career professionals needing development and maintenance of advanced language skills. With this rationale in mind, the University of Hawai'i has created three Web-based courses for advanced study in Chinese and Korean:

- Advanced Web-based Chinese Reading and Writing;
- Advanced Web-based Chinese Listening, Reading and Writing; and
- Advanced Web-based Korean Reading and Writing.

Prior to the development of the Web courses, UH had produced a set of self-instructional CD-ROMs in Chinese and Korean, with some focused on reading authentic texts and some focused on listening (video interviews). The Web-based classes were conceptualized as communities for learners who would benefit even more from the CD-ROMs if, instead of using them on an individual basis, they joined with other learners to engage in preparatory activities before "entering" the CD-ROM, and then followed up with language practice activities following each use of the CD-ROM. The same development process underlay all the courses; this section of the chapter focuses on the development and delivery of the first course, Advanced Web-based Chinese Reading and Writing.

The overall process comprised the following stages:

- Through a series of meetings, the general sequence of instructional activities was designed and revised on paper. (The instructional sequence is described in more detail below.)

- Several popular commercial courseware packages were examined to determine their suitability for enabling the sequence of instructional activities. All were rejected because the team felt it would be impossible to customize them adequately.

- The programmer undertook to design software and databases that would enable all the instructional activities that had been designed within a password-protected environment, employing a three-tier client/server structure based on Allaire ColdFusion® and Microsoft SQL Server®.

- The team worked together to sketch out the site interface, including the placement of activities on pages, the placement of pages in frames, and the placement of menus and navigation guides in the site. The programmer and Web designer determined the file structure for the site.

- While the programmer worked on software development, the instructional designer proceeded with specific design of individual units. After meeting with the other members of the team to incorporate their suggestions, the instructional designer turned over each unit design, roughed out on paper or typed up as a word processing file, to the Web designer. When all units were developed, they were "mapped" onto the instructional period of the coming semester in a syllabus that laid out the entire semester's work schedule and due dates.
- The Web designer converted the paper design into Web pages to fit the course interface, incorporating JavaScripting where needed to enable student self-checking of fill-in-the-blank or multiple-choice answers.
- The Web designer handed over the Web pages to the programmer for the addition of ColdFusion Markup Language (CFML) scripts and incorporation into the course site.
- Team members invited guests into the site before the launch of the course to "wander around" and test the functions in the course. Reported bugs were fixed.
- The course site was prepared for the actual course launch. Student usernames and passwords were created, and a student e-mail list created. Instruction proceeded according to the schedule laid out in the course syllabus.

Pedagogic theory and course development

Without institutional resources for the development of Web-based courses corresponding to the technical support that makes HITS courses possible, the Hawai'i team, comprising an instructional designer, a Web designer, and a programmer, had to rely on its own resources in developing the course. During the development process, these team members with their diverse skills and knowledge worked together, each playing a distinctive role described in more detail below.

The instructional designer was responsible for developing a general sequence of instructional activities that would be followed in all the units, and then developing specific instructional activities for each unit in line with the sequence. The Web designer was actually a language instructor with enough expertise in HTML and JavaScripting to convert the instructional designer's paper version into non-dynamic HTML and to incorporate some JavaScripting for student self-checking of answers. The programmer created and implemented scripts that enabled the dynamic elements of the course, including passwords and permissions, grading functions, student grouping, "word banks," and forums.

While the instructional designer was aware from the beginning of the more obvious constraints of the medium — for example, that the course would be asynchronous and that interactions would be restricted to written communication — he was encouraged by the Web designer and programmer to work without worrying too much about other limitations of the medium. Most of the time, the instructional designer worked on paper to sketch out ideas, which he then revised after meeting with the Web designer and programmer.

The sequence of instructional activities was based on a pedagogic approach grounded in schema theory. Some of the key concepts guiding the design of the course were

- Readers understand a text through a process of interaction between text-based elements (structural and linguistic components) and reader-based elements (behaviors and strategies such as deploying background knowledge and hypothesizing). The most successful readers are those who employ these skills actively and consciously (Barnett, 1989; Carrell, 1988).
- A reader reading alone has access only to his own reader-based elements. A group of readers sharing information can strengthen each other's comprehension and contribute to each other's learning. Creation of community for the sharing of knowledge is vital for good course design.
- An instructional sequence should begin with what students already know, rather than the instructor's assumptions about what learners know. Learning activities should, to the greatest extent possible, be personally meaningful and communicative.

Instructional sequence

In line with the above concepts, the instructional sequence of the course was designed so that each unit comprised the following stages, which are also represented in schematic form in Figure 9.

Warm-up activities/word bank

Students share linguistic and real-world background knowledge by filling out Web-forms with vocabulary and sentences. Student responses are accumulated on a guestbook-page for each query, so that all the answers that have been input are visible at a single glance. Answers are also gathered into a course database — a "word bank" for student use.

Preparatory activities

Students complete a preparatory matching task at the baseline level (rather than the target level) of the lesson. Instant feedback is provided with a "check answers" button employing JavaScripting.

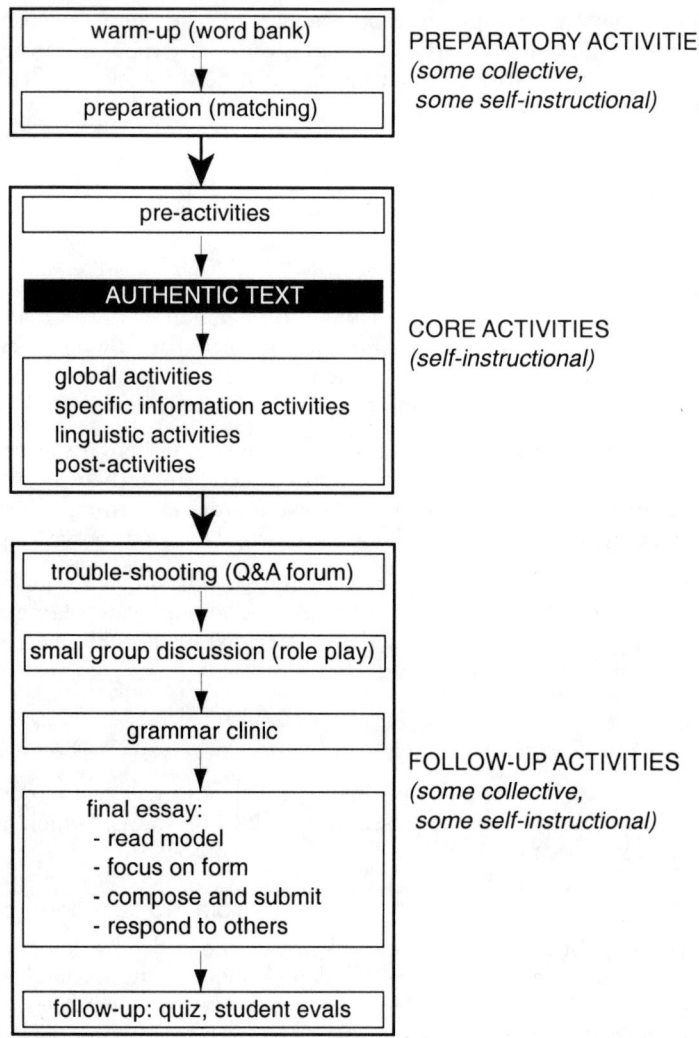

Figure 9. Schematic representation of stages in the UH Web-based courses

Core lesson

Students complete the CD-ROM lesson, which is structured according to a receptive-skill lesson model rooted in schema theory, comprising the following five stages:

- pre-activities — prediction, activating background knowledge;
- global activities — identifying and locating topics, "mapping" the text;
- specific information activities;

- linguistic activities — learning about linguistic forms in the text; and
- post-activities — using the knowledge gained in the lesson in a communicative task that is a natural outgrowth of the text.

Students can then participate in a "Q&A" forum to troubleshoot any problems they had completing the CD-ROM lesson. Discussion can be in Chinese or English.

Students are assigned a discussion task via e-mail. They are directed to a specific thread in the forum, where they interact with one or two other classmates in Chinese in a role-play or task.

After the students have worked on the task, the instructors choose five or six erroneous utterances (i.e., postings that have syntax or usage problems) from the student discussion threads and place them in the next forum, the Grammar Clinic. Students are directed to respond to two or three of the erroneous sentences by supplying a correction. Finally, the teacher adds comments to each thread, and everyone reads over the accumulated contents of the forum.

Post-lesson activities

Students are told in advance of the final writing task of the unit, which is usually a short persuasive essay related to the topic of the lesson. In preparation, students first read a model text on a topic related, but not identical, to the lesson topic, in which certain linguistic features — usually discourse connectors or other useful tools — are highlighted. Students complete linguistic exercises based on the highlighted items in the model text to strengthen their familiarity with these items.

Students complete a final writing task, usually a written role play related to the theme of the lesson, and post the composition to a threaded discussion. Each student is assigned to respond to two other students' writings with appreciations and critiques.

A multiple choice quiz based on the content of the CD-ROM lesson is also included at the end of each unit. The quiz is assigned minimal weight in the grading of each unit.

Additional course elements and teaching tools

To assist students in the management of information resources in the course, including vocabulary that has been posted to the Word Bank, outstanding essays, and useful entries from the Grammar Clinic, the course site also features two management tools: the Course Resource Manager and the Personal Resource Manager. The Course Resource Manager is maintained by the instructor and contains resources for all students, such as the complete archive of Word Bank items. The Personal Resource Manager is unique for each student and contains resources that the student has chosen and placed there. These resources are not contained within the sequence of instructional activities, except that as part of the post-lesson activities students are asked to save or add ten vocabulary items to their Personal Resource Manager that they will use in their final essay.

To assist teachers with monitoring student activity on the course site, managing student usernames and passwords, and assigning grades, the site also includes Instructor Resources. Instructor and student privileges are differentiated such that while the instructor can read and write grades for all students, a student can only view his own grades.

The site also provides access to external informational resources via appropriately placed links to Web-based dictionaries and informational Web sites. In order to look up a word, students need only copy the word from the text at the site and paste it into the dictionary's search field.

In cyberspace, the most difficult thing to replicate is the experience of face-to-face communication. In this course, a sense of community and peer learning is fostered through providing spaces for learner interaction on the course Web site. As each learner moves through the stages of a unit, he passes back and forth from group work environments to an independent environment. This alternation between communal and independent work reflects stages in the learning process as learners and instructor approach the "core" text in each unit and then come back together to react to the text and use the language learned from it. These "core" texts are multimedia reading lessons contained on a CD-ROM, a copy of which is distributed to each student. Each lesson on the CD-ROM is based on an authentic text and follows a sequence of self-instructional activities based on the same pedagogical principles as the course overall.

In comparison with an equivalent course delivered in a traditional classroom format, this reading and writing class offers many more opportunities for the learner to read and write, since only by reading and writing can he communicate. Time devoted to oral discussion in the traditional classroom is turned into time devoted to reading and writing; the targeted modalities are used to teach the targeted modalities.

Initial offering of the Web-based course at UH

The Web-based course was at first offered only to UH Mānoa students as an experimental prototype using an existing course rubric. To gain an accurate image of how the course looked from the students' side, a small-scale case study of the course was conducted, with data gathered through various means. This study is detailed in the following section.

CASE STUDY OF THE WEB-BASED COURSE

Delivering a language course exclusively via the Web constitutes a paradigm shift in teaching; very little relevant research exists to guide the language teaching profession in this new endeavor. How should a Web-based language course be designed and conducted? Will a Web-based language course constitute a valid and legitimate educational experience? How will students respond to and behave in such a course? These fundamental questions guided our investigation in this case study.

We wanted to know if a Web-based language course is viable for students and instructors. We wanted to know more about what learners liked or disliked, and why. We wanted to evaluate students' performance. Under what conditions would they perform well or not perform well? We wanted to know if their language proficiency would improve. To begin to gather information regarding these questions, we systematically observed students' online behavior over a semester during the inaugural offering of Chinese 399: "Advanced Reading and Writing."

Chinese 399 student background information

Student status

According to data provided on the student background survey, a majority of students (9 out of 12) were full-time students at the University of Hawai'i at Mānoa in Honolulu on O'ahu. One student was an instructor at UH. One student worked full time off campus. Another student living on the neighbor island of Kaua'i was retired. The last two students, in particular, were typical distance learners because they were nontraditional students who probably would not have taken the course if it had not been offered on line.

Linguistic background

The background survey also showed that five students in the class were originally from China. All of them immigrated to the US as children and used English as a their primary language. They all spoke Chinese fluently but wanted to improve their literacy skills. An online reading and writing course at the advanced level was ideal for these students.

Motivation for taking the course

Students reported that the instructor's recommendation played a significant role in influencing course selection. A number of students in the online course had taken a traditional course with the online instructor the previous semester and were personally recruited by her for the distance-delivered course. Scheduling difficulty was an additional reason some students reported for choosing the online course. Another Chinese course was canceled at the beginning of the semester, and some students had a problem finding a replacement course to fit their schedule. The online course was ideal for them.

Computer skills

As was expected, the students who enrolled in the online course were computer literate, and most of them reported prior experience using Chinese software. However, most of the students used PC rather than Macintosh computers, and this caused some concerns about the off-line CD-ROM assignments because, at that time, the course CD-ROM existed in a Mac version only. (A PC version has subsequently been developed.)

Rationale for research choices in case study

The aim of this case study of the Web-based Chinese 399 course at the University of Hawai'i was to evaluate the learning environment, the learning experience and learning outcomes (including activities and socialization, as well as measures of understanding and satisfaction). Though there are no widely accepted evaluation criteria for evaluating Web-based learning, one valuable study has been done by Riel and Harasim (1994). In their paper "Research Perspectives on Network Learning," they proposed a strategy for assessment that includes three main areas: network design and structure, social interactions, and individual learning outcomes.

Using Riel and Harasim's model, this case study evaluates the Web-based Chinese 399 course in the following three areas:

- Learning environments
- Learning experiences
- Learning outcomes

Both quantitative and qualitative data were gathered and analyzed. Three surveys yielded quantitative data: a background survey, a post-unit survey, and a course evaluation survey. Qualitative data was obtained from observation, examination of course records, and interviews with the instructor and students.

Learning environment

Design

The design of the learning environment was evaluated in the following areas: course structure and content, learning environment in general, and major course activities. The data in Table 1 show students' reactions to course content and course structure.

Table 1: Ratings on course structure and content (scale: 1 to 5)

statement	mean
The amount of material covered was adequate for the credit received.	4.10
Course content was presented in a well-organized manner.	4.01
A variety of class activities were used to help present course content.	3.94
Examples and illustrations were effectively used by the instructor.	3.92
The instructor used the course Web site effectively for meeting the objectives of the course.	3.85

Note: The mean rating combines satisfaction data from 3 separate administrations of the same survey throughout the semester.

The ratings indicate that from the students' point of view, the course was well designed and well structured, and its content and organization served the course objectives. One student commented, "overall this course is very useful. It is easy to follow, and the structure is clear." Another student said, "[the course] content is challenging and easy to move around [sic]."

Table 2 shows students' evaluation of the learning environment. Students thought that the learning environment was well designed for online learning. At the same time, the mean ratings of 2.72 and 2.39 in Table 2 demonstrate that students did feel a certain degree of distraction and difficulty in understanding online instructions.

Table 2: Ratings on the learning environment (scale: 1 to 5)

statement	mean
The screen layout and interface design of the CHN399 course are consistent and easy to use.	4.16
The design of the Web forums was conducive to discussions.	3.84
The overall learning environment was conducive to learning.	3.79
I tend to get easily distracted in an online environment.	2.72
I had a difficult time understanding online instructions.	2.39

Note: The mean rating combines satisfaction data from 3 separate administrations of the same survey throughout the semester.

Table 3 shows how students felt about the course activities. Among various types of activities, students reported that the most useful part of the learning environment was the forums. Interviews with the students corroborated that students liked the discussion forums. As one student said, "I feel the discussion forum is the best tool in the course, where we can exchange ideas…"

Table 3: Ratings on the course activities (scale: 1 to 5)

statement	mean
The discussion forums (i.e., Q&A, small group discussion) are useful.	3.92
The warm-up activities are useful.	3.91
The Grammar Clinic is helpful.	3.74
The preparatory activities are useful.	3.71
The content of the core lessons (CD-ROM) is well designed.	3.23

Note: The mean rating combines satisfaction data from 5 separate administrations of the same survey throughout the semester.

The learning environment successfully accommodated the pedagogical sequence of activities specifically designed for the course. The close match of Web design and pedagogical design in this customized environment proved conducive to language learning. The forums, which facilitated the exchange of knowledge and ideas among the members of learning community, were particularly critical to the design of the learning environment.

Navigation

Students agreed that the learning environment was easy to navigate and its functions were easy to use. Except for some Chinese input problems that were related to third-party software, the students usually did not have problems doing online exercises, posting messages to the forums, taking online quizzes, and so forth. One student commented, "the course Web site is the best designed that I have had to use. The colors are just right and finding (navigating) information is very easy."

Table 4: Ratings on the learning environment regarding navigation (scale: 1 to 5)

statement	mean
The screen layout and interface design of the CHN399 course are consistent and easy to use.	4.16
I had a difficult time understanding online instructions.	2.39

Note: The mean rating combines satisfaction data from 2 separate administrations of the same survey throughout the semester.

Tracking records showed that students navigated the course in a task-focused fashion. After they logged in, they focused on completing specifically assigned tasks (e.g., write three entries in the warm up activity), and then often left the course. Most of the time they did not routinely navigate to other parts of the class site. For example, there was a news forum for posting announcements, asking questions, and sharing information. However, students rarely went there to check. The consequence was that even if the instructors posted an announcement in the forum, only a few students read it. The instructors had to e-mail the students to let them know there was something new in the course.

Students' task-focused navigation patterns indicate that system developers should employ a task-based approach in designing a learning environment. Developers should anticipate that students may not navigate on their own to ancillary forums and should therefore design approaches to motivate students to explore multiple paths in the learning environment, using different media, such as e-mail, for communication when necessary.

Social interaction: The learning experience

Participation in discussion

Generally speaking, students' participation in discussion was active. When we examined the number of messages posted in forums in each unit, we found that more than half of the students met the requirement of posting at least two messages in a specific discussion task. We also noticed that participation was not evenly distributed. Some students posted comparatively large numbers of messages in certain units but fewer in others. Data from observations, surveys, and interviews indicate that this was due to several factors:

1. Students had varying levels of interest in different units. For example, one student commented of a particular unit, "the unit has been very useful for me. The vocabulary I learned has opened up a new door into Chinese life." As the comment would indicate, the student participated actively in this particular unit.

2. Students had different levels of background knowledge for different lessons, which influenced their participation. In regard to a lesson on Chinese medicine, one student commented, "I wish I knew more about this topic. I wonder [if] it is so important to know about this topic. It seems that it was difficult to discuss this topic and essays about buying medicine. I had [a] hard time to write feedback [sic] on other classmates' essay[s]."

3. Students did not put an equal amount of time into each unit. For example, there was a nontraditional student who needed to go on business trips from time to time, so he did not participate actively on those occasions.

4. If students did not get a response immediately or did not get a response at all from other students, they lost interest in following up. As one student said in the interview, "the level of my motivation went down when I did not get feedback."

Below is an example of uneven participation. The numbers shown in Table 5 indicate that in the forum for essay writing there was an overall higher participation rate in the last two units.

Table 5: Number of messages posted in essay forum

student ID	unit 1	unit 2	unit 3	unit 4	unit 5	unit 6	unit 7	unit 8	total
student 1	4	6	3	4	4	4	14	8	47
student 2	2	2	1	1	3	2	6	3	20
student 3	6	4	4	3	5	5	4	5	36
student 4	9	1	1	4	5	5	10	9	44
student 5	11	4	3	3	4	4	12	5	46
student 6	4	1	3	3	1	0	6	18	36
student 7	7	2	3	4	4	5	6	8	39
student 8	14	5	5	14	8	7	15	17	85
student 9	3	3	1	3	4	3	2	5	24
student 10	5	1	1	3	1	1	5	6	23
student 11	3	3	3	4	6	4	5	10	38
student 12	4	2	3	3	2	4	5	4	27
total	72	34	31	49	47	44	90	98	465

According to observation and students' feedback, there were two major reasons for this unevenness. First, the last two units involved students from Taiwan in a language exchange with the students in Hawai'i. The local students were paired up with Taiwan students so that they could learn Chinese from the Taiwan students, and the Taiwan students could learn English from the local students. Being able to communicate authentically with native speakers sparked students' motivation to participate. As one student commented, "the last two unit[s] were the best. I really like the opportunity to talk to native speakers." Another student said, "I am more confident that I can carry [on] a conversation with a Chinese speaker…"

A second reason for unevenness of participation from unit to unit, and high participation in the last two units in particular, was that the topics of the last two units were celebrities and movies. Students were asked to write a description (local students wrote in Chinese and Taiwan students used English) of a celebrity or a movie and have their language partner(s) guess the name of the actor or movie. These topics and tasks proved to be very interesting to the students. We found that in addition to interacting with their partner(s), many students also participated in the discussion of other pairs to talk about the actors and movies. This extra, voluntary participation also contributed to the high number of messages in these units. The higher participation in the last two units speaks to the importance of designing good tasks, choosing interesting topics, and providing opportunities for students to interact with native speakers in authentic situations.

Student-instructor interaction

Students were generally satisfied with their interactions with the instructor. Table 6 shows the survey results regarding student-instructor interaction.

Table 6: Evaluation of instructor-student interaction (scale: 1 to 5)

statement	mean
The instructors were responsive to students' needs.	4.25
The instructors encouraged student participation.	4.19
Assignments were graded in a timely fashion.	4.17
I felt comfortable contacting the instructors outside class.	4.10
I felt uncomfortable posting questions into the discussion forum.	1.88

Note: The mean rating combines satisfaction data from 3 separate administrations of the same survey throughout the semester.

In this virtual environment, because students and the instructor did not meet face to face, it was crucial for the instructor to monitor the students' learning process, constantly encouraging participation and responding quickly to queries. When the instructor did not provide ongoing structured support, students' participation was not active. An example of this may be found in our experience with the Grammar Clinic.

In the first four units, the instructor limited participation to posting sentences with grammar mistakes and asking students to fix them. The instructor gave no hints or summary of relevant grammar rules. Students felt that they did not get much out of the treatment of grammatical errors, and therefore were not participating actively.

After realizing the problem, the instructor changed the strategy and began to put more effort into interacting with students, offering hints and summarizing grammar points during the discussion. After these changes were implemented, students showed a marked increase in interest. As one student said, "the GC in this unit was much better than the ones before. Dr. Lu was very helpful. She provided feedback quickly. She also gave useful hints and comments."

From this case we can see the importance of instructor guidance in a virtual language learning environment. When designing and conducting a Web-based language course, meaningful communication between instructor and students must be built into the course and actively pursued during instruction; it is a major contributor to student motivation.

Satisfaction with the social interaction of the learning experience

In general, students were satisfied with the social interaction of the learning experience. After finishing the course, most of the students said that they would like to take a similar course in the future. Students also said they would recommend this course to others. Table 7 shows survey results regarding student overall satisfaction with the course.

Table 7: Overall satisfaction with the course (scale: 1 to 5)

statement	mean
I would recommend that other students take similar courses from the same instructor.	4.03
I have a sense of accomplishment so far.	3.76
I enjoyed the learning process and interactions in this class.	3.69
I enjoy getting to know fellow class members.	3.66
The method of course presentation kept my interest high through the entire course.	3.56

Note: The mean rating combines satisfaction data from three separate administrations of the same survey throughout the semester.

According to survey and interview data, students thought Web-based language learning had the following advantages:

1. More flexibility in interaction. Students liked the flexibility of the Web-based course. One student had a full-time job and would not have been able to come to campus three times a week for a class. He said that this Web-based course was perfect for him because he got an opportunity to improve his Chinese using a flexible schedule. Some other students also mentioned that they could log into the course from home at night, which was very convenient. As one student summarized, the advantage of a Web-based course is that "you don't have to be in the classroom at the required time. You can visit the site at any time you want."

2. More interaction in the literacy modalities (reading/writing). Students said that they wrote more in this course compared to their level of writing in a traditional classroom-based course. Because the Web course was largely text-based, there were many more opportunities for students to write in Chinese. A student commented, "I was able to retain more vocabulary over a longer period of time probably because I was using the vocabulary (writing essays or answering questions) almost as soon as I learned it. This is very important for me."

3. More authentic cultural interaction. The Web-based language course provided opportunities for students to interact naturally with native speakers. In the traditional classroom, such opportunities are rare, unless the instructor brings a guest to class or makes a field assignment. The students clearly enjoyed language exchanges with native speakers. This was shown in the high participation rate in the two units that involved native speakers. Examples of students' statements are, "this language exchange is a very good activity...the experience is very valuable." "I truly enjoyed this unit," and "this unit helped me to learn unique vocabulary for discussions with almost any Chinese speaker."

In the context of second and foreign language instruction, and in view of the Internet's tremendous potential to enable transnational and transcultural communication, the students' enthusiasm for interacting with native speakers should be accorded special attention. It appears that maximizing exchange of this sort has the potential to greatly enhance student motivation, which is an important predictor of learning (Crookes & Schmidt, 1991).

Shortcomings in the social interaction of the course

In addition to noting positive things about Web-based language learning, students also expressed their dissatisfaction about some aspects of learning language on line:

1. Lack of adequate sense of community. Students felt that they did not have a true sense of community. Although we did ask students to post their self-instruction and pictures in the first unit, it did not prove to be very helpful for students in getting to know their classmates. One student commented,

   I would like to get know my classmates...Uploading pictures of participants might be helpful if they agreed to be posted on the Web...

2. Lack of adequate sense of feedback. Although most of the students said that they liked the asynchronous approach for this course because it allowed time for thoughtful writing, many students also mentioned that they felt discouraged when they did not receive feedback from others. The students usually did not mind waiting for a day or so for others' responses, but if they did not get feedback after several days or got no feedback at all, their motivation would weaken. As one student said in the interview, "I don't mind waiting a day or so, but it bothers me if I don't get any feedback."

Students' perspectives on Web-based language learning demonstrate the advantages of using the Web for language teaching and learning. The problems of lack of a sense of community and lack of immediate feedback are more related to the nature of asynchronous communication than to particular problems with this Web-based environment. To overcome the drawbacks connected with asynchronous communication, instructors must stimulate students' motivation and to respond students' messages in a timely fashion. The inclusion of a certain amount of synchronous communication in the course (e.g., synchronous Web-based chat during self introductions) may help students get to know each other better.

In an attempt to overcome shortcomings related to community-building, especially, and to enhance social interaction in the course, the instructor tried different approaches to motivate students' participation and to create a positive social dynamic. One approach the instructor used was to raise non-linguistic questions about students' postings. For example, when talking about hotels, one student mentioned that she had previously been to Xi'an, China. The instructor then asked if she planned go to China again, and the student talked about her summer plans. This not only kept the interaction going but also created a friendly conversational atmosphere.

In general, the instructor encouraged students to talk about their personal experiences not only so that would they write more but so that they would come to know each other better. In fact, the instructor often referred to her own experiences when responding to students' postings. In this way, the students came to know more about the instructor as well. Such efforts helped students to overcome somewhat their feelings of isolation.

Learning outcomes

Learning outcomes were evaluated by rating students' essays in an early stage of the course (hereafter called "pre-test") and their essays in a later stage of the course (hereafter called "post-test"), then comparing the ratings. Students were considered to have gained in writing proficiency if post-test scores were higher than pre-test scores.

The evaluation process was as follows:

1. All 12 students' essays in the first unit (self-introduction) were selected as pre-test samples and their essays in the seventh unit (introduction of a movie) were selected as post-test samples.
2. Three Chinese language teachers at UH were chosen to form a professional rater group and three Chinese whose occupations were not related to language teaching were chosen to form a non-professional rater group.
3. In both rater groups, each rater was randomly assigned to rate eight students' essays including both pre- and post-tests of a particular student.

Therefore, each student's pre- and post-test were rated by two professional raters and also by two non-professional raters (See Table 8 for distribution of raters).

Table 8: The distribution of raters (* indicates that the rater rates the student)

	professional raters			non-professional raters		
student ID	rater1	rater2	rater3	rater4	rater5	rater6
student 1	*		*	*		*
student 2	*	*		*	*	
student 3		*	*		*	*
student 4	*	*		*	*	
student 5	*		*	*		*
student 6		*	*		*	*
student 7	*		*	*		*
student 8	*	*		*	*	
student 9		*	*		*	*
student 10	*	*		*	*	
student 11	*		*	*		*
student 12		*	*		*	*

4. Raters evaluated the essays based upon criteria that comprised three areas: vocabulary, grammar, and content, each scored on a scale of 1–5 points. When evaluating an essay, a rater assigned a score for each of the three areas. A rating for an essay was the sum of the scores of these three areas.

5. In each rater group, a rating on each student's pre- or post-test was obtained by calculating the mean of the ratings from the two raters assigned to that student.

6. For each rater group, a one-tail T-test was conducted to compare students' pre-test rating and post-test rating. See Tables 9 and 10.

Table 9: T-test results for pro raters' ratings

	pre-test	post-test
mean	9.677083	12.0625
1-tail probability	0.008834	

Based on professional raters' evaluations, the T-test results show that the average rating of the post-test sample (12.0625) is higher than that of the pre-test sample (9.677083). The test shows that at the significance level of 0.01, the mean rating of the post-test samples was significantly higher than the mean rating of the pre-test samples ($p=0.0008834<0.01$), which indicates an improvement in writing proficiency.

Table 10: Test-test results for non-pro raters' ratings

	pre-test	post-test
mean	9.916667	11.708333
1-tail probability	0.000169	

Based on non-professional raters' evaluations, the post sample also had a higher average rating (11.708333) than the pre-test sample (9.916667). And the T-test results also show that the average rating of the post-test sample is significantly higher than the average rating of the pre-test sample ($p=0.000169<0.01$), which also indicates an improvement in writing proficiency.

THE HAWAI'I WEB EXPERIENCE: LESSONS LEARNED

The most important lessons to be drawn from the University of Hawai'i's experience with Web-based language education fall into two broad areas: *Web course design* and *online behavior*. Web course design refers to the preparation undertaken and the elements put in place before the course is offered, and online behavior refers to student and teacher actions inside the virtual space of the course during the semester. It must be stressed that design and behavior are both vital to the success of a Web-based course. A course that is well designed provides stimulation and guidance to both students and teacher once the course has begun, while a poorly designed course can be confusing and discouraging. Effective behaviors in a Web course create a comfortable social space in which students enjoy customized instruction and have the sense of interacting with real human beings.

These are the most important lessons learned in this project: Web course design must be based on pedagogical principles, and it must focus on being user-friendly. Online behavior must help build a sense of community, and it must create a sense that the teacher is responsive. These "lessons learned" are discussed below. The conclusions offered in this section are based on data gathered from analysis of online behavior as reflected in course postings and tracking records, student feedback surveys, and student and instructor interviews gathered for Advanced Web-based Chinese Reading and Writing (Chinese 399). As learners, students do not have the same awareness of pedagogic processes that teachers do. While teachers are able to reflect on teaching and learning processes using the metalanguage they have mastered through their training, students' awareness generally centers around positive and negative responses to aspects of their learning experience. These responses provide important indicators of the effectiveness of the pedagogic orientation or principle that underlies the course which the students have taken.

Web course design: Pedagogical principles

In the past few years, prepackaged courseware or course management systems such as WebCT and Blackboard have become widely available. Use of these systems, often implemented campus- or system-wide, squeezes instructional designers into a mold established by a generic course management template that is expected to serve the gamut of educational disciplines. The distinct pedagogical needs of language education are not reflected in the design of this generic courseware. For a language instructor seeking to develop a skill-building course, the generic course template provides little guidance toward the development of a good instructional sequence. Entering an "empty" course space in one of these generic course management systems, the designer (who is often the same person who will teach the course) encounters various tools laid out awaiting organization: chat rooms, calendars, quiz modules, and threaded discussion. If time is pressing, the designer may allow the available tools to dictate choices about how instruction will take place. The moment such choices are made, technology has trumped pedagogy, and the designer has abandoned an essential principle: *Pedagogical principles must determine the instructional sequence.*

Table 11: Pedagogical principles associated with Web course design features

pedagogical principle	Web course design feature
Move from what the learner knows to what the learner does not know.	A "collective brainstorming" mechanism, such as a class word bank, comes at the beginning of each unit.
Teach receptive skills before productive skills.	Students work individually with listening or reading materials before doing extensive posting in the course.
Provide opportunities for real communication.	Students engage in a learning exchange with native speakers who log on to the course from the target language environment.
Tailor instruction to student needs.	The Grammar Clinic treats errors that have occurred in student postings in the current unit.
Allow for peer learning.	Students write essays for everyone to read and respond to, not just for the teacher.

While it is a hard fact that choices for instructional activities are constrained by available technology, it is important that the initial stage of instructional design — the composition of the instructional flow — take place apart from any technologically determined template. Ideally, the Web course template — what might be termed the "basic interface" — should be designed to visually reflect the temporal flow of activities, rather than forcing students to jump from page to page trying to locate different tools. Also, if existing software tools do not match the activities the instructional designer would like to include in the course, programming resources should be sought out to *create* the desired tool, unless an effective adaptation of the existing tools can be made.

Table 11 shows some sample pedagogical principles, and the design features of the Hawai'i Web-based courses that conform to each principle.

Course management software may well improve in the next few years, but in the meantime, in order to create courses that adequately reflect sound pedagogical principles, Web course designers who wish to deliver high-quality language instruction may need to plan for intensive investment of resources in programming and Web page creation. If adequate resources are not available, the designer should carefully consider whether or not to go ahead with course delivery. For example, it is difficult to imagine how a prepackaged Web course management system such as WebCT or Blackboard could effectively serve as an effective instructional medium for speaking skills. Intensive investment in programming and design using other Web technologies would be necessary to teach speaking over the Web in a pedagogically sound way.

As an alternative to using the prepackaged courseware mentioned above, the University of Hawai'i developed its own platform for its Web-based courses using self-designed menus and content pages embedded in a frameset. Course content is a combination of static and dynamic Web pages, with dynamic content stored in a database and "fed" to the end user through a set of scripts that enable the various functions of the course. Development of this custom-designed system required substantial investment of time and money and a high level of technological expertise.

In the University of Hawai'i Web-based Chinese course, which targeted reading and writing skills, the only way for participants to communicate was through posting in the forums and the word bank. Since writing was the sole medium of communication in the course, students had many more opportunities to write than they would have had in a traditional writing course. Asynchronous communication reduced pressure on students to write spontaneously and allowed them to think more carefully because they had the opportunity to spend time revising their writing before they sent it out. Other material in the course also required use of the written — rather than the spoken — modality. Data from surveys and interviews reflect students' realization that they did far more reading and writing in this course than they might have done in a similar traditional classroom course. Students felt that this was a strong positive point of the course, which was designed to focus instruction precisely on reading and writing.

Student data reflecting the strengths of this course in maximizing reading and writing practice suggest that the course turned the constraints of the Web-based medium to advantage by *matching modalities:* in other words, matching an available modality (written communication on the Web) to the modality targeted in instruction (reading and writing). These data support the development of courses in which the modality of instruction is similarly matched to the target modality. At present, this means that instruction in speaking would be poorly supported by the Web at any level, but most particularly at the beginning level since students at that level lack even a rudimentary foundation upon which to build.

From the standpoint of contemporary pedagogic practice, using language to communicate is an essential part of the language learning experience. Some of the most important evidence gleaned from the student interviews and surveys in this study points to the importance of person-to-person communication as a critical element of a satisfactory and effective learning experience. Student reaction was especially positive to instructional units in which the learners interacted authentically and naturalistically — that is to say, in which they communicated to exchange real information rather than just to complete a linguistic exercise — with native speakers and classmates in the target language environment. This evidence parallels the emphasis in current language pedagogy on communicative interaction, in contrast with earlier pedagogic models that stressed mastery of linguistic forms.

The evidence gathered in this study strongly supports the conception of Web-based language courses as environments for *communicative interaction* among participants, with language partners, and with the instructor. The evidence does not support models for Web-based courses in which the user interacts primarily with the online material, as for instance in a sequence of self-paced, self-instructional modules.

Modern principles of language instruction place great emphasis on the use of *authentic materials* — that is. materials produced by native speakers for purposes of communication with other native speakers. The CD-ROM-based lessons at the "core" of each instructional unit were all built around authentic materials. Student data from surveys and interviews reflected students' confidence that studying authentic materials would strengthen their capacity to function successfully in the target language environment in the future.

Web course design: User-friendliness

As information-bearing media, Web pages vary in effectiveness due to their content and their presentation. Interesting and well thought-out content is ineffective if poorly presented; poor content cannot be improved by good presentation. As mentioned in the above section on pedagogic principles, pre-planning the instructional sequence before creating course Web pages helps ensure that course content is pedagogically sound and engaging for learners. Once the sequence is well planned, the task becomes to create user-friendly Web pages for effective delivery of the course content.

At the level of the single Web page, principles for sound design are similar to those for print materials: Do not crowd the page with too much text, use visual elements effectively, and so forth. But even more critical to user-friendliness is ease of navigation and use. Students in the University of Hawai'i course were in strong agreement that "the screen layout and interface design of the CHN399 course [were] consistent and easy to use."

Since Web pages have hyperlinks — in other words, "hot" text and/or images that lead the user from page to page through many possible sequences — navigation must be carefully managed to avoid confusion. The University of Hawai'i course employs a dedicated menu bar in a frame on the left side of the browser window that allows users to easily find their way through tasks in the course. The menu bar features expanding menus in each instructional unit, a sequential arrangement of student tasks, and clear geographic separation of course material from ancillary tools, such as online dictionaries (see Figure 10). This presentation of tasks in chronological sequence contrasts with the tool-based arrangement found in most course management software.

Ease of navigation will become even more important in the future, when Web-based components become common in many courses as part of the movement towards distributed learning. Whereas students in CHN399 and other students who voluntarily choose to enroll in exclusively Web-based courses are currently quite Web-savvy, in the future the general level of technical expertise among students using Web-based course components may flatten out. Ease of navigation and use will become even more important to accommodate these users.

Many users have dial-up connections to the Internet and are using older machines and systems. It is important to keep technological demands on the user, such as special plugins and scripting, to a minimum. In the University of Hawai'i course, only one plugin, RealAudio®, was used.

Online behavior: Fostering a sense of belonging

Far from being a tool for self-learning or a "teaching robot," this Web-based course was a locus for meaningful interactions among a group of people. The maintenance and development of this community of learners was an important element of course delivery. Data from this Web-based course suggest that person-to-person communication fostered enthusiasm and sense of belonging, but that a certain social cohesion was still lacking.

The Web enables convenient, almost universal student access, but as of this writing the Web-based environment is unable to approximate the traditional classroom space in the same way that the ITV environment does. Although the Web-based environment does enable learners and instructor to "meet" in a virtual online space, the sense of community is not as immediate as it is in the traditional classroom. For this reason, it is essential to make special efforts to reinforce students' sense of being members of a community of real people.

Student responses to surveys and interview questions in the Web-based course in this study indicated that they felt that the course lacked such a sense of community, and that this affected their level of comfort. They would have liked the chance to get to know each other better outside of the tasks assigned in the course. This data suggests that the creation of social spaces within a course has importance that deserves prioritized consideration alongside the design of tasks and activities more directly related to the learning goals of the course. In response to this feedback, the course designers have, as of this writing, implemented a feature that displays the image of each posting's author alongside the posting, creating an increased sense of interaction with a real person. Moreover, plans for future adaptation of the course include the expansion of areas in the course that are purely social and unrelated to course assignments.

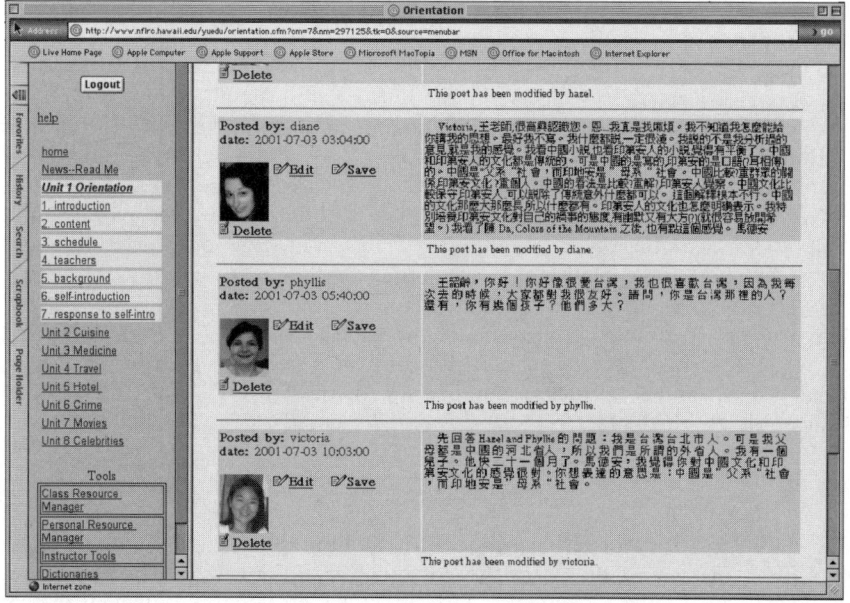

Figure 10. Forum in Web course, showing menu bar at left with expanded unit menu

Online behavior: Instructor participation

In order to accommodate participation by students in any time zone, the communicative environment of this Web-based course was designed to be asynchronous. Participants posted entries at any time for others to read and respond to at their convenience. In a synchronous environment, in contrast, users would all log on at a given time and exchange postings in real time, using such tools as Web-based chat. In a completely open-ended asynchronous environment, users might have to wait an unlimited length of time to get a response to a posting. However, in the asynchronous UH course, interaction occurs within the framework of a regular work schedule requiring a certain amount of participation by a certain deadline. These deadlines encourage prompt response to others' postings.

Data from student interviews and surveys reflected the importance students placed on receiving prompt responses, both from other students and from the instructor. Lack of response to postings was frustrating and disappointing. In the context of an asynchronous course, these data point up the importance of structuring the course schedule in a way that encourages timely responses. The data also indicates the importance of extremely active, intensive participation on the part of the instructor, including prompt response to student postings. Feedback can be tailored and personalized in a dedicated space for real-time reflection and feedback on actual student-produced language. The Grammar Clinic in the University of Hawai'i Chinese 399 course, for example, remains empty until the instructor gathers and analyzes student errors in several discussion threads in the clinic. In each thread, students are invited to "fix" the errors under discussion and to try creating similar examples free of errors. Guidance of the type exemplified in the Grammar Clinic resulted in high agreement ratings from students to statements such as "The instructors were responsive to student needs."

THE ROAD AHEAD

As distance-delivered instruction at UH expands beyond the local community to the national and international community, distributed learning becomes more challenging and presents more opportunities for creative implementation. UH is beginning to explore models where remote learners create their own distributed learning environments by recruiting local tutors, especially conversation tutors, who are linked to and supported electronically by the instructor at UH. Upper level modality-specific courses, such as reading/writing courses, will continue to be developed and offered on line with more modest distributed support, since on-line courses are ideal for developing advanced reading/writing skills. Here, too, however, distributed learning will likely be featured in more and more UH courses as distance students increasingly will be asked carry out field work projects involving local, target-language sources and informants and report on them by carrying out communicative tasks in the learning community on line.

The underlying rationale for distance education is accessibility, making something accessible to someone who would otherwise not be accommodated. For distance-delivered language education to enjoy acceptance and be effective, quality must not be compromised. We at the University of Hawai'i are working to establish accessibility and maintain quality as we advance instruction at a distance in uncommonly taught languages, in particular, to the virtual learning community.

REFERENCES

Barnett, M. (1989). *More than meets the eye: Foreign language reading.* Language in Education: Theory and Practice, no. 73. CAL/ERIC Series on Language and Linguistics. Englewood Cliffs, NJ: Prentice Hall.

Carrell, P. (1988). Some causes of text-boundedness and schema interference in ESL reading. In P. Carrell, J. Devine, & D. Eskey (Eds.), *Interactive Approaches to Second Language Reading* (pp. 101–113). Cambridge, England: Cambridge University Press.

Crookes, G., & Schmidt, R. (1991). Motivation: reopening the research agenda. *Language Learning, 41*(4), 469–512.

Driscoll, M. P. (1994). *Psychology of learning for instruction.* Needham Heights, MA: Allyn & Bacon.

Gower, R., Philips, D., and Walters, S. (1995). *Teaching practice handbook* (2nd ed.). Oxford, England: Macmillan Heinemann.

Riel, M., & Harasim, L. (1994). Research perspectives on network learning. *Machine-Mediated Learning, 4*(2–3), 91–113.

Saltzberg, S., & Polyson, S. (1995). Distributed learning on the World Wide Web. *Syllabus, 9*(1). Retrieved February 19, 2001, from: http://www.syllabus.com/archive/Syll95/07_sept95/DistrLrngWWWeb.txt

Vygotsky, L. S. (1978). *Mind in society: the development of higher psychological processes.* Cambridge, MA: Harvard University Press.

Rhodalyne Gallo-Crail & Robert Zerwekh
Northern Illinois University

LANGUAGE LEARNING AND THE INTERNET: STUDENT STRATEGIES IN VOCABULARY ACQUISITION

Late in 1997, a team of computer scientists and language professionals at Northern Illinois University, in conjunction with Northern Illinois University's Center for Southeast Asian Studies, began development of an Internet site dedicated to the delivery and promotion of Southeast Asian languages and cultures. Today, SEAsite (www.seasite.niu.edu) features materials for both beginning and intermediate students of Thai, Indonesian, Tagalog, and Vietnamese. Funded in part by the National Security Education Program (NSEP), our goal was to build a Web site for these less commonly taught languages that would offer a range of interactive learning resources for Southeast Asian languages, literatures, and cultures. In other words, it was not intended to be purely a language learning site, but rather a globally accessible resource for information about Southeast Asian countries, including instruction in language. Our future development plans call for adding language materials and other resources for Khmer, Lao, and Burmese (again, funded by NSEP).

We knew from the beginning that these Southeast Asian languages are rarely taught in the United States (however, at Northern Illinois University, Thai, Indonesian, Burmese, and Tagalog are taught on a regular basis). To this end, we tried to make each of the four language sites serve as an independent and stand alone introduction to each language and country. Judging by the e-mail we receive, and our online survey questionnaire, our efforts have been a resounding success. People from all over the world use SEAsite on a regular basis. Many are interested in learning one or more of the represented languages, while others are more interested in the history, culture and religion, or politics of the countries. Our users range from serious students of the languages, to those who wish to learn some Tagalog, for example, so they can communicate with a spouse or friend. High school and college teachers and students, business people, military personnel, and our own language students at Northern Illinois University are all part of the world wide SEAsite audience.

Although the site was designed to be independent of any formal classroom instruction for the languages, the language professors who teach these less commonly taught languages at Northern Illinois University routinely make use of the resources and interactive language exercises as part of their classroom instructional efforts. These resources include, among others, readings in the second language often accompanied by spoken audio, online dictionaries for three of the

---

Gallo-Crail, R., & Zerwekh, R. (2002). Language learning and the Intenet: Student strategies in vocabulary acquisition. In C. A. Spreen (Ed.), *New technologies and language learning: Cases in the less commonly taught languages* (Technical Report #25; pp. 55–79). Honolulu, HI: University of Hawai'i, Second Language Teaching & Curriculum Center.

languages, and a variety of Java applets that provide interactive tools for learning vocabulary, testing comprehension, and constructing written answers in the target language, in both roman and non-roman orthographies.

Both NSEP and our SEAsite team became interested in assessing more formally the ways in which our students were using these Web-based resources. Did the use of Web-based instructional tools help them in mastering language concepts? Could our students learn, for example, new vocabulary words with better retention if they used the Web-based resources? Which of the Internet resources did our students find most useful or most helpful sin their study of a second language?

This chapter describes the results of a semester long case study that we conducted among 20 students studying Tagalog at Northern Illinois University. The case study specifically was interested in assessing how these students used different learning strategies with different Web-based tools as they studied new vocabulary words and how this affected their success in learning and mastering the new vocabulary.

INTRODUCTION

Recent studies in second language vocabulary learning indicate that certain learning strategies are more effective in acquiring new vocabulary words (e.g., Brown & Perry, 1991) and that students have preferences in the strategies they use to learn vocabulary words in a second language. Learning efforts that combine a semantic processing strategy and a keyword strategy when studying new vocabulary words, for example, promote more vocabulary acquisition than a keyword or semantic mapping alone. These studies also indicate that using these strategies simultaneously enables students to become more effective in acquiring new vocabulary words with different levels of difficulty. These studies, however, have only compared two or three different strategies for vocabulary acquisition and have not shown an overall picture of the optimal use of learning strategies for vocabulary learning.

Most of these studies also constructed test instruments that used traditional forms of testing vocabulary retention, word depth and appropriate word use; for example, wordlist, defining words, and multiple choice on paper. These studies have not used any computer-based or Internet-based assessment tools.

This case study describes student strategy use of five different learning strategies that were supported by Internet-based activities. In addition, we measured achievement using Web-based quizzes and we collected the information about student preferences and quiz scores in a data base.

RELATED LITERATURE

Learning Strategies are the special thoughts or behaviors that individuals use to help comprehend, learn, or retain new information (O'Malley & Chamot, 1990). The effective use of learning strategies is believed by many in the field of language acquisition and pedagogy to be one of the most important skills that students need to master in order to achieve success in language learning. Learning strategies are important to language learning because they enhance students' own learning, and students use them for active, self-directed involvement that is essential for developing communicative competence (Oxford, 1990).

Generally, strategies are categorized in several ways; for example, metacognitive, cognitive, memory, compensation, affective, and social (Oxford, 1990). Metacognitive strategies involve thinking about the learning process, planning for learning, monitoring of comprehension or production while it is taking place, and self-evaluation after the learning activities have been completed. Cognitive strategies are more directly related to individual learning tasks and entail direct manipulation or transformation of the learning materials (Brown & Palincsar, 1982). Strategies under this category include formally practicing with sounds and writing systems, recognizing patterns, analyzing expressions, translating, taking notes, and summarizing. Social strategies are cooperative learning activities that involve peer interaction to achieve a common goal in learning (Slavin, 1983) and to ask questions for clarification. Strategies under this category may include the ability to cooperate with peers, cooperating with proficient learners, developing cultural understanding, and becoming aware of others' thoughts and feelings. Affective strategies as described by Oxford include "lowering your anxiety, encouraging yourself and taking your emotional temperature" (p. 17). Compensation strategies are used to overcome limited skills in speaking and writing. Students may use gestures, frequently ask for help, coin words, and in some instances avoid communicating in the target language (p. 19).

Oxford (1996) has argued that a greater emphasis should be placed on identifying effective language learning strategies and on teaching students how to use them successfully. Many have reported the differences between successful and less successful learners based on the language learning strategies they use (e.g., Abraham & Vann, 1987; Chamot & El-Dinary, 1999; Cohen & Cavalcanti, 1990; Lawson & Hogben, 1996; Naiman, Frohlich, Stern, & Todesco, 1996; Vandergrift, 1997). Good language learners seem to be skillful in monitoring and adapting different strategies. They demonstrate flexibility in using strategies to accomplish different language learning tasks. On the other hand, poor learners cling to ineffective strategies that hinder successful language learning. They focus too much on details, whereas effective learners focus on the task as a whole (Chamot & El-Dinary).

Kojic-Sabo and Lightbrown (1999) cited the following conclusions in their study of students' approaches to vocabulary learning and their relationship to success:

- More frequent and elaborate strategy use was associated with higher levels of achievement.

- Lack of self-reported effort on a student's part was linked to poor performance.

They cited time and learner independence as the two most closely related successful elements for a high level of achievement in vocabulary learning. Thus, if students spend more time on their own using effective strategies in a given language task, language learning will be more successful.

In Gu and Johnson's (1996) study of vocabulary learning strategies and language learning outcomes of Chinese students learning English as a foreign language, they concluded, "that both direct and indirect approaches to vocabulary learning can be useful" (p. 668). The direct approach includes oral repetition of words, reading words in context and employing a wide range of strategies in learning. Approaches they found ineffective, and which were overused by the group of students who did not perform well in the study, included a memorization strategy and putting greater emphasis on visual repetition of word lists.

The study reported here is a preliminary investigation of the vocabulary strategies students used in learning Filipino/Tagalog as a foreign language and their relationship to vocabulary learning achievement. This study is different from previous studies on language learning strategies because "technology," that is, the Internet, was the medium for gathering the data and presenting the strategies, as well as the vehicle for testing student performance over a semester of learning a foreign language.

PURPOSE OF THE STUDY

This case study of students studying Tagalog at NIU using SEAsite addresses the following questions: What learning strategies are used by students to acquire new vocabulary in a second language? What strategies facilitate longer retention, depth of word knowledge, and appropriate word use? What are the implications of these results in the teaching and learning of vocabulary words in a foreign language classroom, particularly when the medium for presenting instruction is, in part, the Internet?

This chapter describes the different learning strategies that our students used for vocabulary acquisition; compares these strategy groups as categorized by Oxford (1990) and identifies the most effective ones that were used to acquire new vocabulary through the use of two language assessment tools found at www.seasite.niu.edu/Tagalog that tested word retention, depth of word knowledge, and appropriate word use; and discusses pedagogical implications of the use of strategy-based activities on the Internet.

PARTICIPANTS

Participants in the study were 20 college students who were at the beginning level of learning Tagalog/Filipino as a foreign language at Northern Illinois University. Table 1 shows the profile of each of the students based on the Strategy for Language Learning (SILL) Questionnaire Version 5.1 (Oxford, 1990), which was administered to all the students at the beginning of the semester. The SILL is designed to provide a profile of English speakers who are learning a new language. This questionnaire helps students think more about their previous language learning experiences and helped us create an initial profile of each student's language learning capabilities based on their reported use and awareness of various language learning strategies. The scores reported are based on a scale of 5.0 and are our students' averages for each of the strategies covered in the SILL Questionnaire. Although the strategies profiled in the SILL questionnaire are not linked to any specific task, such as learning new vocabulary, the questionnaire does help to provide an initial assessment of how well a particular student might be expected to do in learning a new language.

Table 1: SILL student profiles

student	remembering	use mental processes	compensating	organizing/ evaluating	managing emotions	learning with others	average
1	3.4	3.3	2.2	3.5	3.8	4.0	3.4
2	2.9	3.4	3.6	3.2	2.4	4.2	3.3
3	2.9	2.0	4.0	2.6	2.4	3.8	3.0
4	3.7	4.4	3.7	1.7	2.1	4.4	3.5
5	2.6	2.5	3.3	2.8	3.0	3.0	3.0
6	3.0	3.8	3.0	4.0	2.0	4.0	3.3
7	2.6	1.8	1.3	1.7	1.2	2.3	2.0
8	2.9	3.2	4.1	3.1	1.6	3.2	3.1
9	2.6	2.4	2.5	2.6	3.0	2.4	2.1
10	2.8	2.6	4.3	1.4	3.3	2.1	2.5
11	3.3	3.4	3.7	3.8	3.1	4.6	3.6
12	3.1	3.5	3.5	3.6	3.3	3.8	3.5
13	3.3	3.1	3.3	3.9	3.4	3.5	3.4
14	2.7	2.7	3.3	2.3	2.0	2.1	2.6
15	3.2	3.2	3.7	3.3	3.1	3.0	3.2
16	4.5	5.0	4.8	4.8	4.7	4.8	4.8
17	3.7	2.6	3.6	2.9	1.7	3.4	3.0
18	3.7	3.8	3.3	3.4	2.3	3.7	3.3
19	4.0	3.9	3.5	4.3	4.1	5.0	4.1
20	3.7	3.1	4.4	4.4	2.9	4.2	3.7

Six main strategies are covered in the questionnaire. *Remembering more effectively* is a memory strategy characterized by, among others, making associations, placing new words in context, using imagery and sound and image combinations. *Using mental processes* is a cognitive strategy that reflects repeating, practicing with sounds and writing, practicing the new language in a variety of authentic situations, using references, and so forth. *Compensating for missing knowledge* is a compensation strategy that allows students to use all possible clues to guess meaning, to understand the overall meaning and not just single words, and to find ways to get the message across. *Organizing and evaluating learning* is a metacognitive strategy that gives students the ability to link background knowledge to newly acquired knowledge, to set goals and objectives, to plan for a language task, and to learn from errors. *Managing emotions* is an affective strategy that helps students to be positive about themselves and their learning. Often students will keep their own "learning log." *Learning with others* is a social strategy that encourages students to work with peers, develop cultural awareness, and be willing to ask for and accept correction during language tasks.

Table 2 shows two groups of students based on their overall average on the SILL questionnaire. The average for cluster 1 indicates that students "generally used" all the learning strategies covered in the SILL, while the cluster 2 group average indicates that students "sometimes used" the learning strategies, but not very often. As the clustering indicates, only 6 of the 20 participants used all of the learning strategies and were aware of these modes of learning while 14 demonstrated an average, if not minimal, use of these strategies. This initial profiling of the students from the SILL Questionnaire helped provide a benchmark of expectations about their performance in the class. Those who indicated a greater awareness and use of the various language learning strategies would be expected to perform better than those who lacked these traits.

The minimal use of strategies by cluster 2 is an indication that these students need to be made aware of the different foreign language learning strategies that can be used in the learning process. They also need to be trained explicitly in how to use these strategies more effectively. Several studies (e.g., Green & Oxford, 1995) have shown that the active use of strategies helps students attain higher proficiency in the target language and perform successfully in other language tasks. Therefore, foreign language training should include strategy instruction early in the language learning process. We believe that both the classroom and the Internet can provide innovative and meaningful materials that demonstrate different strategies and their use in foreign language learning.

Table 2: SILL questionnaire grouping

cluster	overall average
1 (6 students)	3.7
2 (14 students)	2.9

DATA COLLECTION AND ANALYSIS

Data collected in this study included classroom observation made by the language instructor, weekly reports made by students in their accountability chart, interviews made by the instructor with the students, an online (Web-based) strategy survey, and online tests. Cohen (1987) and Cohen & Hosenfeld (1981) argued that learning strategies are internal mental processes and not directly observable behaviors; their identification and description have relied greatly on students' reports (cited in Chamot & El-Dinary, 1999). However, most language strategy research has favored the use of questionnaires, inventories, and surveys because information can easily be collected by a large number of participants and the analysis is uncomplicated (e.g., Cohen, 1998, O'Malley & Chamot, 1990, Oxford, 1990, 1996).

Students participated in classroom activities four days a week and one day was designated for activities in the language center for audio and computer-based Internet activities. The instructor also designed *classroom* activities that demonstrated the different strategies used in this study. Sample activities included telephone relay, Pictionary, role-playing, charade, a concentration game using words and pictures, reading short cultural narratives, and paired/small group conversation. To record weekly activities, students were asked to keep an accountability chart that indicated which strategies they used at home and on the Internet, the time spent on each strategy, and the activities that they preferred in the classroom. The accountability chart was used during teacher-student conferences. As part of the required tasks for this class, students were asked to visit the Web site and to study on their own at home during the week. When at home, they kept track of the different ways they studied a weekly list of vocabulary words and kept track of the amount of time they spent studying those words. When visiting the Web site, students were asked to choose any of the five strategy-based activities presented on the Tagalog Web site. Each vocabulary lesson was presented with Web-based activities that supported the following strategies:

ASSOCIATION

This is a *memory strategy* that involves associating new language information with familiar concepts. It helps strengthen comprehension as well as make new vocabulary words easier to remember. We used the matching exercise pictured in Figure 1.

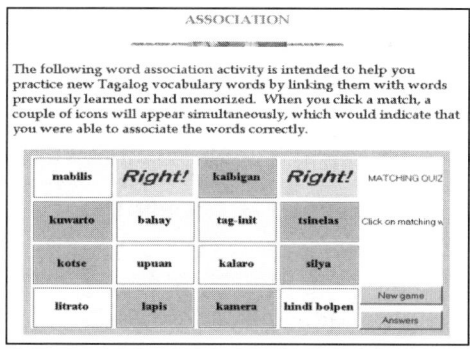

Figure 1. Java-based word matching exercise

TRANSLATION

This is a *cognitive strategy* that allows learners to use their own native language as a basis for understanding new vocabulary words in the second language. This strategy is helpful early in the language learning process. This was supported by the flashcard exercise shown in Figure 2.

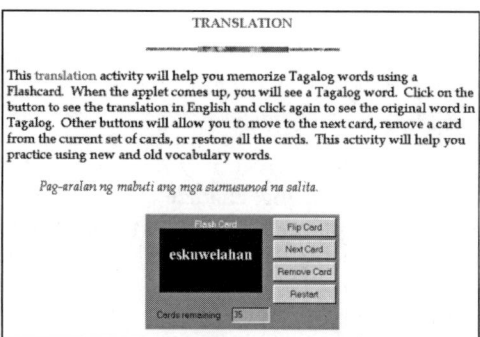

Figure 2. Java-based flashcard exercise

USE OF LINGUISTIC AND OTHER CLUES

This *compensation strategy* utilizes previous knowledge of the second language, the learner's own language, other languages learned, and other sources that are not language related to provide linguistic and other clues to the meaning of new vocabulary words. Students read second language sentences (with accompanying spoken audio) and had access to an online Tagalog-English dictionary for this activity. Figure 3 shows is a screen snap shot of a typical "clues" page.

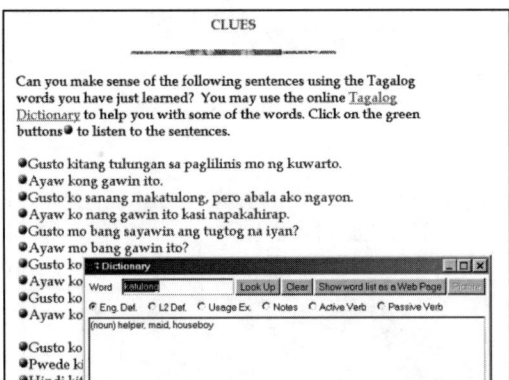

Figure 3. Clues page with the movable dictionary window on top

DEVELOPING CULTURAL UNDERSTANDING

This *affective strategy* provides learners with some background knowledge of the culture for a better understanding of new vocabulary words. Students read text that supplemented the weekly theme (e.g., "Ownership and Possession") with a discussion of Filipino attitudes, beliefs, and cultural traditions related to this topic. The discussion often used the weekly vocabulary words in context.

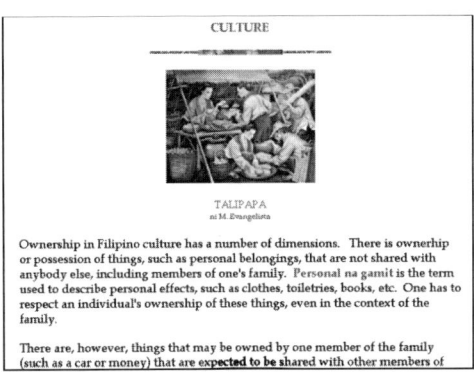

Figure 4. Cultural essay related to weekly theme

OVERVIEW AND LINKING WITH ALREADY KNOWN MATERIAL

This metacognitive strategy involves reviewing new vocabulary words for an upcoming language activity and linking these with what the learners already know.

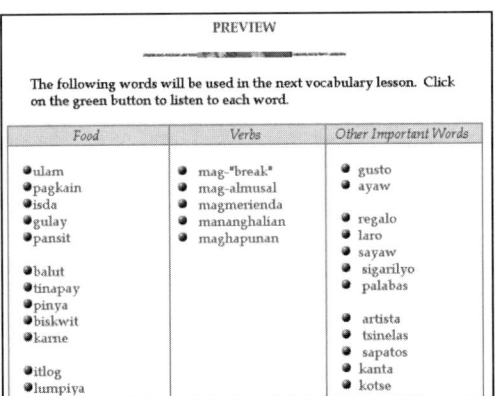

Figure 5. Preview of next weekly theme

As mentioned, the Web-based activities included flashcard, word matching, and an online dictionary, as well as picture-drag-and-drop and sentences with audio. All of these activities except the last are Java applets that provide considerable interactivity with a student. Prior instruction on how to use these applets and activities was demonstrated in the classroom and at the language center. Additional instruction was also available on the Web site. Each week, students chose any activities that suited their individual style of learning. As part of the reporting process, students also filled out an online strategy survey to assess the strategies they used most, those they found most useful, and those they enjoyed the most.

An online quiz and an e-mail quiz were administered to the students at the end of each week to measure their progress. The online quiz was an Internet-based quiz that combined multiple choice, fill-in the blanks, and short answer items. These items tested word definition and appropriate word use. The e-mail quiz combined appropriate word use in sentences and word depth. Students were presented with pictures on the Internet and asked to describe each picture or write a short narrative about any topic of choice using the pictures presented and the weekly vocabulary words. Vocabulary words included in all the tests were based on the weekly thematic lessons presented in class and from all the exercises posted on the Web site. Answers elicited on the tests were evaluated by determining acceptability; for example, synonyms were accepted.

Student answers to the online quiz questions, as well as their overall score, were recorded each week in a database along with their weekly strategy survey answers. A copy of the online survey appears in the Appendix. Descriptive statistics were used to provide a quantitative analysis of the data collected.

RESULTS, DISCUSSION, AND ANALYSIS

As noted before, descriptive statistics were used to cluster the students into two groups based on their average SILL scores, a self-reporting tool that helped provide an overall profile of our student participants. As noted before, cluster 1 students demonstrated a greater and more diverse use of strategies while cluster 2 students showed a more infrequent use of strategies and reported using similar strategies at all times. Given this distinction between the two groups, one would expect that the cluster 1 students would demonstrate more potential in the classroom.

We also determined the mean, median, and standard deviation of the student quiz scores and these results helped us group the students into two new groups that we will call G1 and G2. The G1 group scored above the mean quiz score and the G2 group scored below the mean quiz score. These new groupings were then used in a cross tabulation analysis of the online survey results where the students reported which learning strategies they used during each week of the case study. This cross tabulation showed a preliminary relationship between vocabulary learning strategies used, achievement level, and the initial SILL grouping of students. Students who belonged to the initial cluster 1 SILL group turned out to be the same group of students whose quiz scores were above the mean, and those students who were in the initial cluster 2 SILL group corresponded with the group whose quiz scores fell below the mean. This demonstrates that students who are more familiar with different learning strategies and who frequently used a wider variety of strategies achieved greater success in learning new vocabulary words than those who did not.

Students in both groups (G1 and G2) reported in their accountability charts that they spent approximately 3 to 5 hours a week doing the Web-based exercises. This result is understandable since students were required to spend at least 3 hours each week on these exercises as well as other related language tasks at the language center; for example, listening to tapes and studying Web-based thematic lessons.

Most of the students in G2 reported that they spent a similar amount of time at home memorizing lists of words and writing the words repeatedly in their notebooks. On the other hand, G1 students reported less time at home (not more than an hour) reviewing lists of words, using words in sentences and writing these words on small notecards.

Kojic-Sabo and Lightbrown (1999) indicated that time and learner independence are two closely related factors for high levels of achievement in language learning. But they also added that the use of effective strategies helps language learning become more successful. Although G2 students reported more time spent on both the Web-based and at-home language learning exercises, they unfortunately used less effective strategies such as writing lists of words repeatedly and memorizing them outside of meaningful contexts. G1 students reported a similar amount of time doing Web-based exercises, but less time doing language learning tasks at home. They, however, used more effective strategies at home such as using the words in meaningful sentence construction and organizing word cards. This same group also demonstrated more interest in using the Web-based exercises effectively.

Supporting information based on instructor observations, student accountability charts, interviews, and the written e-mail quizzes supports a similar conclusion. Students who reported a more varied use of strategies were those who performed well on their quizzes and demonstrated more word retention and better command of the language. This is an important indication that using a *variety* of strategies in language learning contributes to a student's language achievement.

This observation has important implications for instructional design, particularly if the instructional material is going to be presented over the Internet. Students should be provided with a variety of learning aids, even when doing something as simple and straight forward as learning new vocabulary. It is not sufficient only to publish a list of words and their other language mates on the Internet and expect that students will study them and learn how to use them correctly in sentence construction. Our case study has shown that providing a wide variety of different learning aids that support different learning strategies has a more pronounced impact when it comes to word retention and word depth.

ONLINE QUIZZES

Thirteen weekly Web-based quizzes were administered to the participating students. The quizzes became available online just prior to the scheduled time to take the test, thus the students did not have an opportunity to take an early look at the quiz and gain an advantage. The quizzes combined multiple choice, fill in the blank, and short answer type questions. Thus, they were primarily used to measure word definition and appropriate word use. The quizzes were automatically graded when submitted by a student, and the results of each student's quiz was saved in our database. A sample quiz is included in Appendix. A number of the students indicated that they had not taken any tests on the Internet before and expressed concerns about using this mode of testing. This expression of anxiety supported what was uncovered in the SILL questionnaire regarding one's ability to manage emotions in language learning. Students reported an average of 2.0, which is an indication that they have a very low use of their affective strategies. This anxiety level may have affected the scores of some of the 12 students (see Table 3) that fell below the mean (see Table 4). However, after a couple of weeks, the participants seemed to lose their anxiety over taking Internet-based quizzes. Familiarity with them, as well as giving them access to similar Web-based "practice" quizzes, lessened their concerns. The practice quizzes were identical in format to the real quizzes. When submitted, a page would appear in the browser that showed them their answers to each question along with the correct answers. Thus, they had immediate feedback on their effort.

As remarked earlier, the group of students who scored above the mean quiz score were, for the most part, the same group of students who were grouped into the cluster 1 SILL group. Those who reported (in interviews, accountability records, and online surveys) using a wider variety of learning strategies were those who consistently performed better on the quizzes. These are the same students who, in their interviews and accountability records, indicated initially that they were less concerned with taking quizzes online and using Internet-based learning resource.

Table 3: Students' quiz scores

scores below the mean n=12 (female=5 male=7)	scores above the mean n=8; (female=5 male=3)
128	204
125	199
116	182
115	153
114	152
111	138
110	137
101	132
91	
82	
75	

Table 4: Students' overall scores

	N	minimum	maximum	mean	SD
total score	20	75	204	129.65	34.97
valid N	20				

VOCABULARY STRATEGIES USED

Initial comparison of the two groups of students indicated some similarities in their use of the five different strategies. (see Appendix C) Both groups indicated that the clues activity (which demonstrates how the vocabulary words are used in sentences and provides audio for all of the sentences) is the one they used the most and found very useful, followed by association (an activity that requires students to rely on background knowledge to remember previously learned words) and translation (much like using a bilingual dictionary). In addition, both groups also indicated that they enjoyed doing association and clues the most. The choice of activities was probably influenced by the expectations of the instructor, that is, students were expected to be able to use the vocabulary words in context and to identify the meanings of words used in context. In addition, both groups indicated that they spent most of their time doing the translation and association activities, but this was to be expected since these two activities naturally required more time to complete. The only difference was how they ranked the strategy they used most. G1 group preferred the use of association, culture, and clues as the top three choices, and G2 ranked translation, association, and clues as the most used strategies. The students in the G2 group reported that the translation activities were similar to using a bilingual dictionary. Although translation is helpful in the early language learning process, it can also slow the development of other vocabulary related language skills, such as using words appropriately and in meaningful contexts. On the other hand, association as a memory strategy can strengthen comprehension as well as make new vocabulary words easier to remember.

CONCLUSION AND PEDAGOGICAL IMPLICATIONS

This case study has indicated that strategy use plays a very important role in language learning, especially in learning vocabulary words. Our data showed that the more diverse the strategies chosen to assist in language learning, the more our students retained and recalled new vocabulary words. This is also related to the conclusions made by Craik and Lockart (1972), that the more diverse and profound the processing involved in the learning, the more effective and long term the learning is likely to be.

SEAsite employs a wide variety of instructional tools that offer considerable flexibility for language teachers to use in ways that support a number of learning strategies. In other words, our site is not a typical "point-click-see" Web site. We have substantial qualitative evidence that the language students like the variety of ways in which they can approach their learning tasks. In particular, they like the activities that are interactive and provide visual feedback. Future Web development efforts, whether at Northern Illinois University or other locales, should strive to provide a mix of activities that permit students to be flexible in their study habits and which engage the students on multiple cognitive levels.

Another factor that contributed to greater achievement is having some prior knowledge of the language. Students who had exposure to the language even before they enrolled in the class, that is, students of Filipino Heritage, achieved higher scores than those who came to the class with no background at all. This is not surprising. Five of the eight participants that were above the mean are Filipino Americans, that is, Filipinos born in the US. Of the six Filipino American students in the class, only one fell below the mean. This individual student expressed no knowledge of the language at the beginning of the semester.

According to language learning studies cited in Carter and Nunan (2001), there are several factors that may affect a student's strategy use. The following are some of the factors that we believe influenced the choice of strategies the participants used in the classroom, on the Web, and at home:

- Motivation for learning the language was an important influence on their choice and use of strategies. Most of the participants who fell below the mean on the quizzes took Tagalog only to fulfill their foreign language requirement. In their reported strategy use, they often used associational memory strategy, and translational cognitive strategy, to learn their vocabulary words. They used the other three strategies, clues (compensation strategy), culture (affective strategy), and overview (metacognitive strategy), only minimally. On the other hand, the students who fell above the mean all indicated high interest in the language. Most were of Filipino heritage and desired to learn and speak the language. Some took the class to fulfill their foreign language requirement, but also to meet others from the Filipino culture. These students all expressed interest in achieving a high grade. They also reported a more diverse strategy use. They reported equally using association, translation, and the other three strategies, clues, culture, and preview of the next lesson.

- The language-learning environment affected the strategies used. Unlike learning in a second language setting, the participants did not have a community where they could interact with others beyond the four walls of the classroom. Although the participants were encouraged to work in groups for doing work outside the classroom, most of them reported that they worked individually rather than in groups.

    We believe that the use of the resources on the Internet helped contribute to this kind of isolation. When someone is reading something on a computer monitor, whether it's a news story from CNN or a second language reading on SEAsite, it is far too easy to tune others out and to remain isolated with one's thoughts. Perhaps this is an indication that some instructional resources that are going to be placed on the Web should be designed specifically to be done as group activities. The Tagalog site on SEAsite does have a chatroom where students can log in and communicate with one another in written Tagalog. From time to time, one of our Tagalog speakers will join the chatroom and provide assistance on points of grammar and sentence construction. A discussion forum is also available for those who would like to post a question or a statement that pertains to the target language and have other users respond to the posted inquiry. Resources such as these may encourage students to work with one another in a more group oriented endeavor.

- Some differences in strategy use and achievement in vocabulary learning were also seen along gender lines. In this study, more female participants were above the mean than their male counterparts. They also reported that they were willing to try different strategies in learning the vocabulary words on the Web, at home and also in class. However, male participants reported that they spent more than 4 hours on the Web studying the vocabulary words each week while the female participants reported only 1–2 hours per week of Web site activities.

- The nature of the language task presented to the participants, that is, vocabulary learning using different strategies, was new to most of them. Most were not aware that there actually were different ways of learning vocabulary words. Some expressed uncertainty about which strategy would work best for them. Most preferred memorizing and writing the words in their notebooks in order to learn the new words each week. Others felt the need to keep weekly word lists written on small pieces of paper. Most of the participants also expressed uncertainty of how best to use the Web site.

The applied nature of the study meant that certain controls possible in other classroom and Internet-based research were not possible in this case. First, students visited the Web site and did the lessons on their own or with a group without the instructor's presence and were only required to report their activities using the online strategy survey and in their accountability calendar.

Second, some participating students reported difficulties navigating the Web site. This problem may be due to students' inability to focus on the assigned tasks or unfamiliarity with the site. Inability to focus may be related to the following variables: a) open access to other sites while on line, b) failure to open the vocabulary activities on the Web with a java-enabled browser, and c) the absence of immediate supervision and assistance from the instructor when difficulties or questions arose. Unfamiliarity with the site can be attributed to students' limited access and use of the site for language learning purposes. A number of students reported that using the Internet as a learning tool was a new and unfamiliar concept for them. This is a significant observation in its own right. Using the Internet to study is, in many ways, still a relatively new idea for many students. For many, the Internet is a medium that provides entertainment and e-mail. It is clear that future use of the Internet in our language classes calls for more training of students in how to navigate and how to use the online resources. Perhaps a published "user's guide" on the site itself, that explains what to do and how to proceed, is something that we need to investigate and initiate.

Although the results described here are preliminary findings, they helped us accomplish several things. First, we recognize the need to train students in the use of strategies. Strategy training should help students learn to use a variety of methods to learn weekly vocabulary lists. Several studies (e.g., Cohen, Weaver, & Li, 1996) have suggested that explicitly discussing, describing, and reinforcing strategies in the classroom can promote greater achievement in language learning. Although this study did not intend to determine whether strategy-based instruction should have a role in foreign language learning, we strongly believe that if we introduce and emphasize strategies that can promote achievement in language learning, students will improve their performance on any given language task, for example, vocabulary learning.

Second, instructional materials for classroom implementation and Internet use should be centered around building strategy techniques. Brown (1994) stated that in developing activities and materials for classroom and individual student use, more attention should be paid to specific instructional goals. Examples of such goals are to help students lower their inhibitions, encourage risk taking, and to promote cooperative learning. We hope to consider goals such as these in developing and improving the materials in the Tagalog Web site and to provide more interesting and meaningful classroom activities for learning Tagalog as a foreign language.

Third, we identified some limitations in learning using the Internet. Students need more time to acclimate to how to study using the Web and how to use the online resources efficiently. More time needs to be spent in the first week or two with personal instruction on how best to use the language Web site. In addition, occasional computer program glitches or technical difficulties developed and technical staff worked to limit future problems. Problems of this nature sometimes frustrate one's attempts to study and work with the online materials.

Fourth, we were able to begin discussing more efficient and reliable techniques using active server pages to track student strategy use while accessing the Internet in real time. This will help us make better judgments of reported versus actual use of the online materials. Finally, we have begun to explore statistical methods for analyzing the quantitative data in such a way that it will lend further support to the qualitative data that we derive through observation and interviews.

REFERENCES

Abraham, R. G., & Vann, R. J., (1987). Strategies of two language learners: A case study. In A. Wenden & J. Rubin (Eds.), *Learner strategies in language learning* (pp. 85–102). Englewood Cliffs, NJ: Prentice Hall.

Brown, H. D. (1994). *Teaching by principles: An interactive approach to language pedagogy.* Englewood Cliffs, NJ: Prentice-Hall.

Brown, T. S., & Perry, F. L. Jr. (1991). A comparison of Three Learning Strategies for ESL Vocabulary Acquisition, *TESOL Quarterly, 25,* 655–670.

Brown, A. L., & Palincsar, A. S. (1982). Inducing strategy learning from texts by means of informed, self-control training. *Topics in Learning and Learning Disabilities 2,* 1–17

Carter, R., & Nunan, D. (Eds.). (2001). *The Cambridge guide to teaching English to speakers of other languages.* Cambridge, England: Cambridge University Press.

Chamot, U. A., & El-Dinary, B. P. (1999). Children's learning strategies in language immersion classrooms. *The Modern Language Journal,* 83 (3), 319–338

Cohen, A. D., & Cavalcanti, M. C. (1990). Feedback on composition: Teacher and student verbal reports. In B. Kroll (Ed.), *Second language writing: Research insights for the classroom* (pp. 155–177). Cambridge, England: Cambridge University Press.

Cohen, A. D., Weaver, S. J., & Li, T-Y. (1996). *The impact of strategy-based instruction on speaking a foreign language.* Unpublished manuscript, National Language Resource Center, University of Minnesota.

Cohen, A. D. (1987). Studying learner strategies: How we get information. In A. Wenden & J. Rubins (Eds.), *Learner strategies in language learning* (pp. 31–40). Englewood Cliffs, NJ: Prentice Hall

Cohen, A. (1998). *Strategies in learning and using a second language.* London: Longman.

Cohen, A. D. & Hosenfield, C. (1981). Some uses of mentalistic data in second language research. *Language Learning, 31*(2), 285–313.

Craik, F. I. M., & Lockart, R. S. (1972). Levels of processing: A framework for memory record. *Journal of Verbal Learning and Verbal Behaviour, 11,* 671–684.

Green, J. M., & Oxford, R. (1995). A closer look at learning strategies, L2 proficiency, and gender. *TESOL Quarterly, 29*(2), 261–297.

Gu, Y., & Johnson, R. K. (1996). Vocabulary learning strategies and learning outcomes. *Language Learning, 46*(4), 643–679.

Kojic-Sabo, I., & Lightbrown, P. M. (1999). Students' approaches to vocabulary learning and their relationship to success. *Modern Language Journal, 83*(2), 177–191.

Lawson, M. J., & Hogben, D. (1996). The vocabulary learning strategies of foreign language students. *Language Learning, 46,* 101–135.

Naiman, N., Frohlich, M., Stern, H. H., & Todesco, A. (1996). *The good language learner.* Clevedon, England: Multilingual Matters.

O'Malley, J. M., & Chamot, U. A. (1990). *Learning strategies in second language acquisition.* Cambridge, England: Cambridge University Press

Oxford, R. L. (1990). *Language learning strategies: What every teacher should know.* New York: Newbury House.

Oxford, R. L. (Ed.). (1996). *Language learning strategies around the world: Cross-cultural perspectives* (Technical Report #13). Honolulu: University of Hawai'i, Second Language Teaching & Curriculum Center.

Slavin, R. (1983). *Cooperative learning.* New York: Longman.

Vandergrift, L. (1997). The comprehension strategies of second language (French) listeners: A descriptive study. *Foreign Language Annals, 30,* 387–409

APPENDIX A: TYPICAL WEEKLY ONLINE QUIZ
text only

DESCRIBING SOMETHING GOING ON

1. Choose the most appropriate response to this question: Ano ang ginawa mo sa karne?
   a. Hiniram ko.
   b. Niluto ko.
   c. Ininom ko.
   d. Binasa ko.
2. Write what you will do with a "book."
3. Write the incompleted aspect of "to return."
4. Write the completed aspect of "to drink?"
5. Write the contemplated aspect of "to do."
6. Write the incompleted aspect of "to wipe."
7. Write the completed aspect of "to launder."
8. Write the contemplated aspect of "to cook."
9. Write the completed aspect of "to buy"
10. Write the incompleted aspect of "to throw."
11. Choose the best possible answer to this question: Ano ang gagawin mo sa sulat?
    a. Kakainin ng nanay ko.
    b. Ibibigay ko sa kaibigan ko.
    c. Hihiwain ko ng maliliit.
    d. Isasara ko mamaya.
12. Write what you will do with a glass of milk.
13. _____(to buy, completed) ko ang sapatos na maganda sa Mall.
14. _____(to mix, completed) niya ang bawang, karne at suka sa kawali.
15. _____(to crush, contemplated) mo ang bawang bago ihalo sa karne.
16. _____(to carry, incompleted) nila ang mga libro sa opisina.
17. _____(to use, completed) ng titser ang mga estudyante sa kanyang "lecture."

18. _____ (to reach out for, completed) ng sekretarya ang mga papel sa ibabaw ng mesa.

19. _____ (to ask for, contemplated) ng mga anak ang pera para sa bakasyon.

20. _____ (to water plants, incompleted) ng dyanitor ang mga halaman sa aming opisina.

[send]

APPENDIX B:
TAGALOG VOCABULARY STUDY WEEKLY SURVEY

1. For this week's lesson, please rank the five learning strategies you used on a scale of 1 to 5. 1 indicates you used it *the most*, 5 indicates you used it *the least*.

   Association [1 ▼]
   Translation [1 ▼]
   Clues [1 ▼]
   Culture [1 ▼]
   Preview [1 ▼]

2. For each of the five learning strategies, use the following scale to report how *long you spent* using each strategy this week:

   1 = not at all
   2 = less than 30 minutes
   3 = 30 minutes – 1 hour
   4 = more than 1 hour

   Association [1 ▼]
   Translation [1 ▼]
   Clues [1 ▼]
   Culture [1 ▼]
   Preview [1 ▼]

3. Please rank the *usefulness* of the five learning strategies you used this week on a scale of 1 to 5. 1 indicates you found it very useful, 5 indicates you found it not to be useful at all.

   Association [1 ▼]
   Translation [1 ▼]
   Clues [1 ▼]
   Culture [1 ▼]
   Preview [1 ▼]

4. Please rank the *enjoyability factor* of the five learning strategies used this week on a scale from 1 to 5. 1 indicates you found it very enjoyable. 5 indicates you found it not to be enjoyable.

   Association [1 ▼]
   Translation [1 ▼]
   Clues [1 ▼]
   Culture [1 ▼]
   Preview [1 ▼]

[submit survey]

APPENDIX C: STUDENTS' LEARNING STRATEGY USE

Table 1. Strategy ranked highest in use

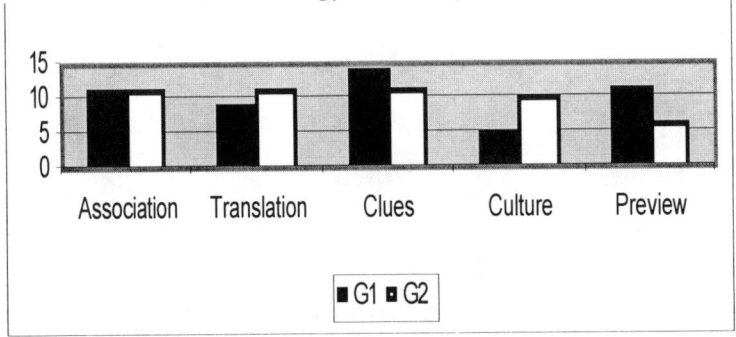

Table 2. Strategy ranked second highest in use

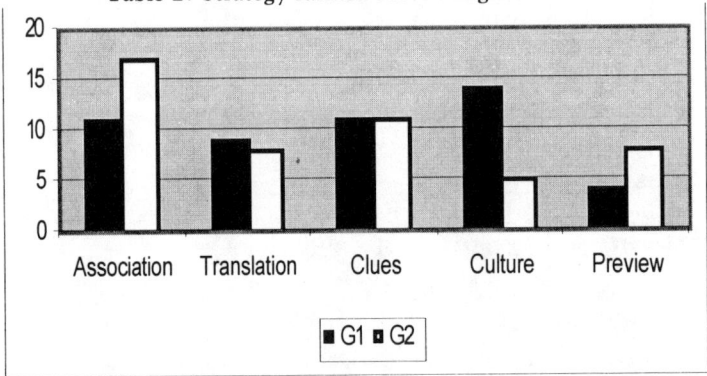

Table 3. Strategy ranked third highest in use

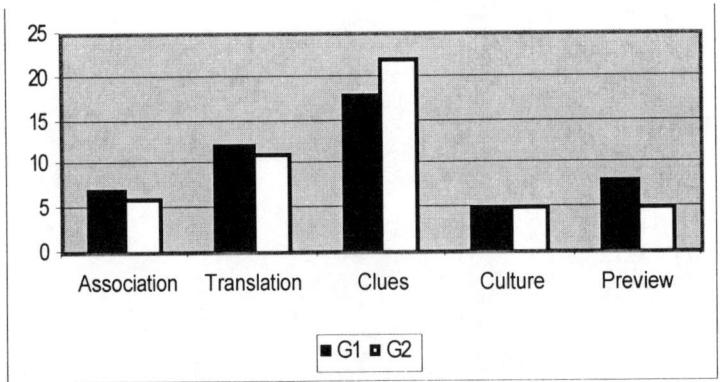

Table 4. Strategy on which most time was spent

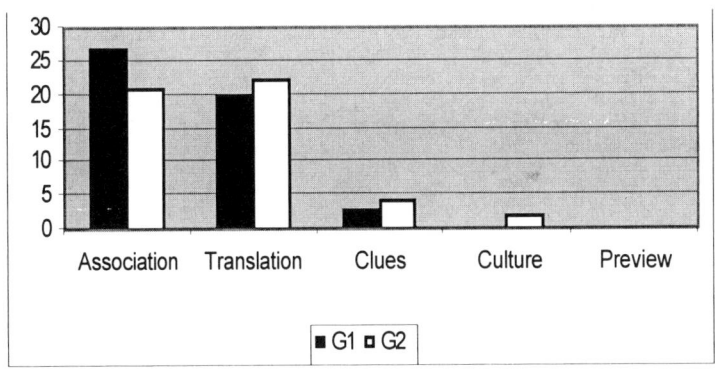

Table 5. Strategy on which second most time was spent

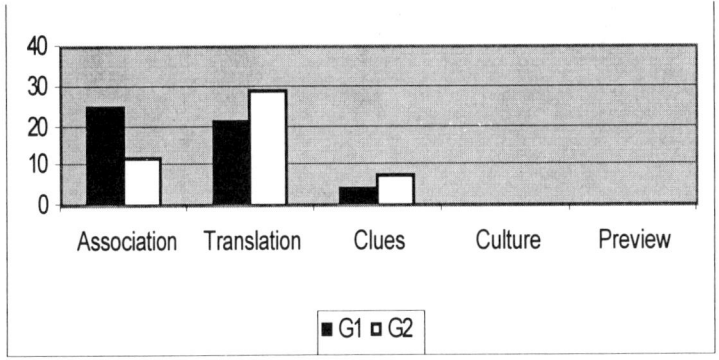

Table 6. Strategy on which third most time was spent

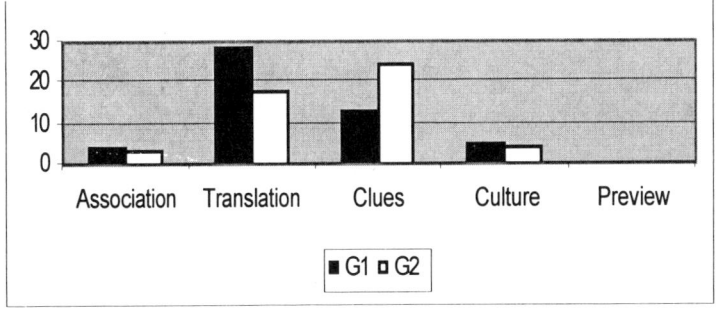

Table 7. Most useful strategy

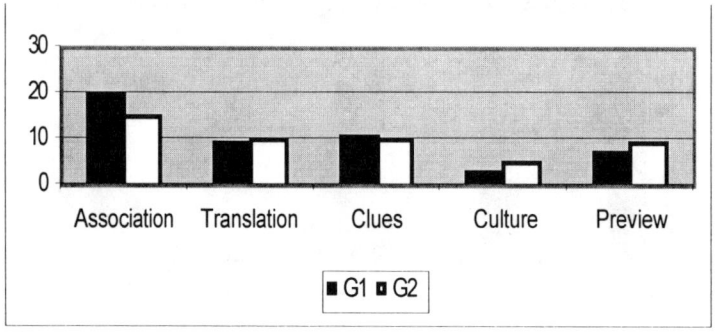

Table 8. Second most useful strategy

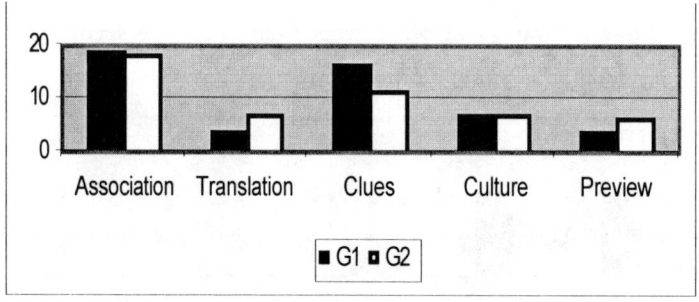

Table 9. Third most useful strategy

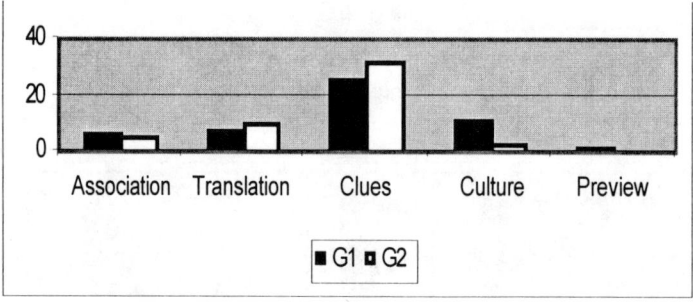

Table 10. Most enjoyed strategy

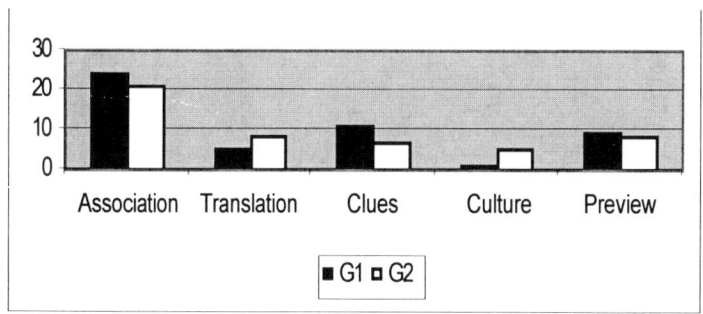

Table 11. Second most enjoyed strategy

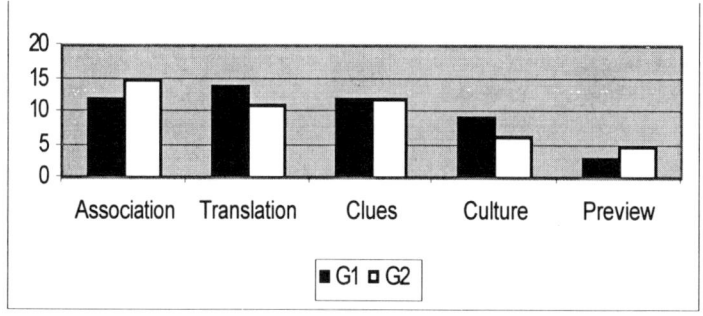

Table 12. Third most enjoyed strategy

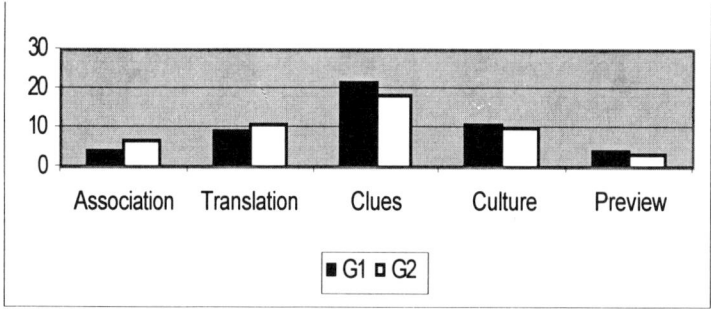

Ken Petersen
American Council International Education

VIDEO IN THE VIRTUAL LANGUAGE CLASS: BUILDING A MODEL FOR WEB-BASED INSTRUCTION

OVERVIEW

The Internet is steadily transforming the nature of information acquisition and distribution as its depth and potential become manifest. Educators and administrators have responded to this newly expanded learning environment by investing significant resources in the technology of distance education. The cost of developing quality computer-based materials and curricula — in both time and money — can prove prohibitive for many who attempt to take advantage of the promise offered by the technology. It is essential that the lessons learned in the trenches be shared with others who are engaged in the struggle. In this light, this case study will examine not only the technical victories and defeats that have led to the development of the video-based Central Asian language modules at www.cenasianet.org, but also the resources necessary to implement such a program.

With support from the National Security Education Program (NSEP), a consortium of organizations — headed by Indiana University and including the American Councils for International Education (ACIE) and SCOLA[1] — has been engaged in the development, test-teaching, and distribution of Internet-based language learning modules for four critical languages of the Caspian/Central Asian region: Azeri, Kazakh, Turkmen, and Uzbek. The modules are targeted at both classroom-based and self-directed learners of these languages who are functioning at the intermediate and advanced levels of proficiency. In the case of the Turkmen language, novice level was also included in the target group. The American Councils was responsible for the design and elaboration of the modules as well as the sourcing of authentic broadcast materials from each of the four countries. Indiana University piloted the modules in conjunction with its Inner Asian and Uralic National Resource Center's intensive summer immersion program, while providing review and test teaching of all the modules, evaluation, and project oversight. In further support of the program, SCOLA contracted with the project to introduce regularly scheduled news broadcasts to universities and other subscribers to supplement the Internet-based modules with news broadcasts in each of the target languages. The goal of the modules, which use pre-recorded versions of the SCOLA news broadcasts, is to provide training to help learners develop the

---

[1] SCOLA is a non-profit educational consortium that receives and re-transmits television programming from more than fifty different countries in their original languages.

Petersen, K. (2002). Video in the virtual language class: Building a model for Web-based instruction. In C. A. Spreen (Ed.), *New technologies and language learning: Cases in the less commonly taught languages* (Technical Report #25; pp. 81–95). Honolulu, HI: University of Hawai'i, Second Language Teaching & Curriculum Center.

strategic listening competence required for comprehending unedited news broadcasts. To a lesser degree, the modules support reading and speaking skills, as well as provide cultural commentaries.

Since January 1999, the publications team at the American Councils has been engaged in developing this unique resource for teachers and learners of Central Asian Turkic languages. The end product of these efforts is the Web-based CenAsiaNet video module series. Built around six hours of authentic news broadcasts from Azerbaijan, Kazakhstan, Turkmenistan, and Uzbekistan, the modules offer a broad range of activities to help students comprehend the dense, rich language with which they are presented. They also offer a unique opportunity for students to work with authentic materials in these critical languages.

Each video clip is accompanied by a fully developed set of activities that are designed to help the student prepare for the specific content of the clip and to assist him in processing and comprehending what he has seen and heard. The activities include drag-and-drop matching and categorization drills, multiple choice, true and false, and fill in the blank activities. (see Figure 1)

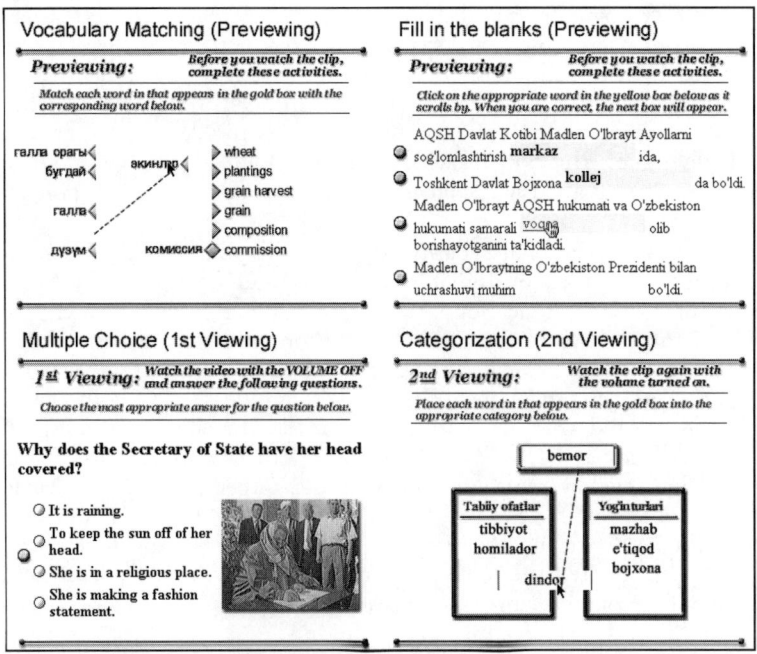

Figure 1. Task-type examples

This study focuses primarily upon the pedagogical as well as the technical considerations in the development of the project's Internet resource. It also provides a brief overview of the process of materials acquisition and Web-content development.

PEDAGOGICAL CONSIDERATIONS

The development of CenAsiaNet required strategic planning for both the methodology as well as the logistics of the project. These "lessons learned" provide important insights into the development of less-commonly taught language curricula and using authentic materials as the basis for instruction. The project team first had to resolve several pedagogical issues before developing the CenAsiaNet modules. These included

- the acquisition of materials;
- the development of Web-based language-learning activities for languages with non-Roman alphabets and no standard fonts;
- the creation of pedagogically sound activities to cultivate accurate structural, sociocultural, and strategic listening comprehension skills for authentic materials — a long-standing problem for the teaching of any foreign language; and
- the solicitation of feedback from teachers and students engaged in classroom use of the modules.

MATERIALS ACQUISITION

In keeping with contemporary approaches to teaching for proficiency, which stress the development of students' communicative competence in a foreign language, the core audio materials for CenAsiaNet were selected from authentic news broadcasts and obtained through SCOLA. This approach allowed the project team to choose from a variety of immediately available materials, while avoiding the often complex and expensive process of obtaining copyright permission for foreign-language broadcasts. This provided the development team at American Councils with more time to devote to the development of activities.

Methodologically, the greatest challenge would come from the content of the material itself. Central Asian newscasts tend to be dry, monotonous monologues with little to no visual support. Relevant supplementary materials in any of the language are also scarce — making it difficult to enrich the video materials. For example, the Turkmen broadcasts were particularly difficult to adapt because of the lack of visual support, which is typical of the Turkmen media in this era of post-Soviet authoritarianism. The broadcasts were delivered almost exclusively by "talking heads," with an occasional ceremonial prop in the background that had little or nothing to do with the topic of the broadcast. Creating language-learning activities and exercises to accompany such unmodified discourse proved to be perhaps the most challenging pedagogical aspect of the project.

For each of the four languages, a native-speakers were employed to create the linguistic content for the activities that accompany the video broadcasts. In many cases, these native-speakers worked on the project from their homes in Central

Asia. This meant that the development team was faced with having to coordinate material development with writers who had little to no computer knowledge and, occasionally, no e-mail access. In addition to the logistical difficulties that this situation created, the writers' lack of familiarity with computers posed some pedagogical problems as well. The tasks created by the materials developers were often quite appropriate for a classroom environment, but needed considerable modification to fit within a network-based paradigm. The team at ACIE is staffed with language educators and L2 speakers of Central Asian Languages and was thus able to make necessary modifications on site rather than having to continually send the materials back to the developers. Nonetheless, this editorial work greatly slowed down the production process.

DEVELOPMENT OF WEB-BASED ACTIVITIES

To adapt broadcasts of Central Asian languages produced *by* native speakers *for* native speakers to the learning needs and expectations of American students posed quite a few challenges for writer-developers. For all modules, native speaker language course developers were used, but, in many cases, their proficiency in English was poor. In order to help them understand how speakers of English — the projected target student population — would learn most effectively, the project team consulted with them extensively.

An additional, related problem facing the developers was how to prepare Web-based materials in languages with scripts that have no standardized fonts.[2] To solve this dilemma, the American Councils created a custom set of Central Asian fonts to be used in the Internet modules (See "Technical Considerations" below).

CULTIVATING STUDENT PROFICIENCY IN LISTENING

Due to the fact that American students traditionally experience the greatest difficulty in developing their listening skills — more so than speaking and nearly always more than reading — in most nondiglossic foreign languages, the project coordinators considered the effective teaching of listening comprehension skills one of its most important goals. Most of the materials available via SCOLA could best be used through adapting tasks (as opposed to adapting texts) to the intermediate and advanced levels of foreign-language. Given the varied availability of novice level language-teaching materials among the four target languages, the team proceeded on the assumption that students using the Uzbek and Kazakh broadcasts on CenAsiaNet would have some prior knowledge of the language. For Turkmen and Azeri, however, this assumption could not be made. Therefore, novice-level activities were developed to accompany the broadcasts in these languages. Even

---

[2] A commercially-produced font (*TransCyrillic*) exists that includes the character sets of all of the Central Asian languages, though it carries with it a price of approximately $150. In order for a student to read the materials in the target language, she would be required to purchase the font. Thus, it is not a viable solution.

with the inclusion of adapted tasks for novice learners, it is likely that the unadapted listening texts would be difficult for most students.

The activities themselves largely focus on specific aspects of communicative competence, aiming to help students develop the knowledge and strategies they would need to comprehend these and similar broadcasts. In specific, these include structural, socio-cultural, and strategic competence. Structural competence — in this case, vocabulary — is critical when the learner has no clues other than a stream of words that he may use to interpret meaning. The CenAsiaNet modules, therefore, teach essential vocabulary in pre-listening activities to "prime" students to understand the coming audio texts. Students are then given the opportunity to listen to the broadcast, using these essential already-practiced lexical items as scaffolding to assist with comprehension. Other types of pre-listening activities encourage student prediction about the content in the video clip, which also helps students to contextualize the authentic texts. Throughout the activities, socio-cultural competence[3] is reinforced through cultural information provided to students via accompanying cultural commentaries. Of all the components of communicative competence, strategic competence is likely the most important in listening to authentic materials. CenAsiaNet's pre-listening and listening activities focus both on the development and use of strategies for listening.

In addition to developing specific skills and competence, the activities have been fashioned to facilitate retention of the language that is processed during viewing. Each module is organized according to a consistent model. Learners begin by previewing all the questions for a particular in advance, setting up expectations for their sentient memories. They are then instructed to view the clip without sound (using visual memory), whereupon they are presented with a battery of questions based on the visual cues that are presented in the video. Still shots from the video frequently accompany the questions in this section. The questions themselves ask students to use deductive reasoning, based upon what they have seen, to describe what is happening, where it is happening, who is involved in the events, and so forth. Thus, by the time the volume has been turned on and the floodgate of language released, students should have a solid framework around which they may begin building deeper comprehension. The final step is viewing with sound (using auditory memory). Students may then view the video as often as is needed to answer the battery of questions which guide them towards comprehension of the clip.

There is a significant amount of flexibility built into the modules. Students may re-listen when they need to, back up and start over, go on to another module before finishing a previous one, and control their paths through the modules in many other ways, as well. The computer notes these various choices for each student in tracking his progress (accomplished through recording of scores). In this way, students who are using the CenAsiaNet modules have full control over how they approach and

---

[3] Socio-cultural competence can be roughly defined as understanding those aspects of culture that are needed for comprehension of interactions at a given level — in this case, at the novice, intermediate, and advanced levels.

use the modules. A by-product of this flexibility is the accommodation of individual differences. The learner is able — through his or her choices — to learn in the way that best suits his or her learning style(s). For example, random learners can choose to do the clips in any order they choose. Sequential students can work in order from the first clip to the last clip.

The team also believed it was important to reduce learner anxiety and to make the modules enjoyable for students. The team attempted to reduce anxiety in two ways. First, students have a considerable amount of control over the approach and manner in which they use the modules and their progress through them, as described above. Second, after completing a module, students can choose whether or not to have their scores recorded. If they would be more comfortable re-doing the module, then they can choose not to record the score. They can then work their way through the activities again, likely with greater precision. To make CenAsiaNet fun for students, news broadcasts were chosen with the most interesting visual support available and activity types have been varied to require both cerebral and mechanical activity on the part of students.

WORKING WITH TEACHERS AND STUDENTS

The modules have been built to accommodate both independent learners as well as students and teachers who are incorporating the online activities into their course materials. The independent learner benefits from the pedagogical guidance and tips on viewing strategies, as well as the judgmental feedback provided in the activities. In this way, the computer fulfills a portion of the role that would otherwise be played only by a teacher. The classroom students also benefit from these features, though they have the opportunity of receiving more detailed feedback and guidance from their instructor. For these students, tools for scorekeeping and communicating with the course instructor have been built in: By allowing the teachers to review their students' progress, the modules let the teachers know where the class is having difficulties and which video clips may require further work.

TECHNICAL CONSIDERATIONS

In order to deliver the materials and content developed for CenAsiaNet, several important considerations were made in selecting the proper technological tools and architecture. University faculty and Web-course developers are often unaware of the distinctions between competing technologies and the benefits of choosing one over another. Below we offer some advice and experience for programmers, administrators, and language faculty in designing Web-based programs for the LCTLs. This presentation of lessons learned is not meant to endorse any particular product or technology, rather it is to illustrate a variety of issues to consider when selecting from different technology options

The most daunting challenge presented by the CenAsiaNet video modules was the question of video delivery. The project set out to create Internet-based language-learning materials built around a series of 30-minute news broadcasts in the four target languages. Given that all of the activities in the modules were to focus on the comprehension of the language presented in the news broadcasts, the quality of the video could not be compromised too severely by compression. Yet, uncompressed, a 30-minute video clip commands upwards of 10 gigabytes of disc space. In all, the combined length of all the video in the project is a full 6 hours in length (three 30-minute newscasts for each of the four languages). Thus, it was critical that the technical team develop a viable, flexible strategy for delivering video that would be Internet deliverable and yet maintain a level of quality high enough to assure its effectiveness as the primary text for building language activities.

The first step taken was to break each video down into several smaller clips. Each broadcast was, for pedagogical as well as technical reasons, divided into five to six individual clips lasting approximately 5 minutes a piece. The second step was to keep the physical dimensions of the digital video display as small as possible. Following extensive testing of viewability and file size ratios, a standard screen size of 176 x 144 pixels was reached. What remained was to select a video format and several levels of audio and video compression to cater to the various levels of bandwidth through which users are able to access the video.

STREAMED VS. DOWNLOADED MEDIA

There are two video formats that account for nearly all Web-delivered video: RealMedia and QuickTime. Each has considerable benefits as well as its share of shortcomings. For the sake of helping identify the factors that informed CenAsiaNet team's choice of video format, a brief analysis of these two standards is in order. RealMedia files are extremely compact digital media files that employ streaming technology to facilitate faster broadcast over the Internet. Streaming media is defined by RealNetworks, the creators of RealMedia technology, as follows:

> Streaming media allows you to send small packets of information over a network connection. The user receives the information packets and plays [your] media piece by piece. The process is almost invisible to the user except for a small amount of buffering at the beginning.[4]

What this definition fails to mention, however, is that the media stream relies upon sufficient performance from the Internet, the end-user's ISP, the phone line, the modem, and, finally, the computer's hardware and software configurations.[5] If any link in this chain breaks down, the media presentation falls apart. Even on

---

[4] *What is Streaming Media? RealProducer Plus User's Guide.* (1998–2000). Retrieved July 1, 2001, from
http://www.service.real.com/help/library/guides/producerplus85/htmfiles/preparin.htm#13313

[5] Internet service providers are often congested due to heavy demand; some telephone lines do not support the required data rates; some modems may be inadequate (below 28.8) or simply will not perform adequately (if a download rate is less than 20 kilobits per second or 2.5 kilobytes characters per second, the user will have difficulty playing the RealMedia presentations).

broadband connections, net congestion can cause video and audio transmission to pause, break, and skip. RealMedia also offers little in the way of navigability within any given video clip. If the user wants to move forward or back through a clip, he does so blindly: the act of moving the position slider freezes the video on the current frame and the user must guess where to release the slider. Once released, the initial buffering begins anew and the user must wait to see where in the video he has landed. While avoiding a lengthy initial download, the user is only able to work with the video in the small "packets" in which it is delivered.[6]

QuickTime media files, on the other hand, download in their entirety to a temporary location on the user's hard drive — taking significantly more time to load, yet assuring a single standard of quality and allowing the user to repeatedly review the downloaded file and even save the file permanently. QuickTime is also able to compensate for slower load time by supporting progressive downloads, which allow part of a movie to be displayed before all of its data has been received over the network. Confronted with net congestion or less than adequate hardware configuration, the only consequence is additional download time — yet, the quality of the media remains intact. This factor, above all, led to the choice of QuickTime as the video format for the delivery of the CenAsiaNet broadcasts.

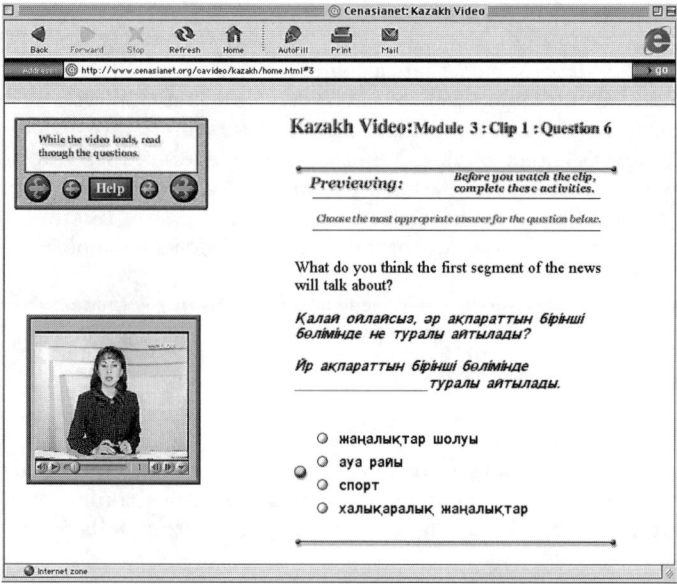

Figure 2. An example of the CenAsiaNet learner interface

---

[6] This is not to say that RealMedia is an inappropriate choice for the development of any language materials. When the media serves as supplementary materials or is small enough in length to be easily replayed, RealMedia can be an effective method of delivery.

QuickTime offers several other features that make it very desirable for the purpose of language instruction. First is the ability to allow the user to jump to specific points in the video. This is done either through the use of chapter tracks[7] or by specifying a start time that begins playing the movie at a designated frame. The QuickTime plug-in also embeds cleanly into a Web page and does not require a separate helper application to launch. This allows the video to be seamlessly integrated into a coherent design framework (see Figure 2). The student is able to operate the video controls within the same window as the activities. RealMedia also has an embeddable plug-in, but in testing has proven prone to drastic browser/platform inconsistencies.

VIDEO COMPRESSION

With QuickTime established as the standard video format, testing began on an appropriate compression scheme. A battery of sample files was produced, posted to the Web, and reviewed by the CenAsiaNet editorial board. The 5-minute test files ranged from 20 to 1.2 Mbs and represented a broad range of quality. Response from the board members reflected the disparity in bandwidth that is currently endemic to the entire medium. Those who accessed the files from university Ethernet connections insisted on the high quality standard that loaded instantly on their machines. Those working from dial-up connections at home responded in frustration that anything over several megabytes was prohibitively slow to load.

It was evident that a compromise needed to be sought by offering users two different levels of quality: one highly compressed, for those bringing the video in over a phone line, and another of higher quality for those with broadband access. The high-end video was compressed using the Sorenson codec with a spatial quality level of 50%. A frame rate of eight frames per second was found to allow the video to play with relatively smooth flow of motion and very little loss of quality. The audio was processed with an IMA 4-to–1 compression at a sampling rate of 22.050 Hz. The low-end video was also compressed using the Sorenson codec, but with a spatial quality level of just 20%. The frame rate was also cut to just one frame per second. The result is that the video is clear, but maintains a slide-show quality. In the audio, however, there was no room for further loss. The exact same audio compression scheme was employed on the lower quality video. The resulting files sizes for the high-end video clips range from 8 to 13 Mbs; the low-end clips range from 1 to 2.5 Mbs. Each video clip takes an average of approximately 5 minutes to load. Here, the pedagogical design dovetails effectively with the technical design; during the download, the student is engaged in the previewing activities for the clip (which should take at least five minutes to complete).

---

[7] For a detailed explanation of how chapter tracks work, see: http://www.apple.com/QuickTime/products/tutorials/chaptertracks.html

FONT CREATION

The languages included in the CenAsiaNet project presented the next major challenge — that of font selection. Three of the four target languages were, at the time of production, in the process of converting from Cyrillic to Latin-based scripts. As work on the project began, only Azerbaijan had made decisive strides in adopting the recent orthographical transformation. Turkmen and Uzbek still seemed to be vacillating between the old and new scripts. Thus, the decision regarding the most appropriate script for students to work with was not clear-cut. To help inform the decision, the question of font selection was posed to a number of Central Asian scholars and was the topic of lively debate at the annual Central Asian Studies Workshop in Madison, Wisconsin, yet no consensus emerged. The choice was finally left up to the materials developers themselves. When the script questions were resolved, three distinct fonts needed to be created: Turkmen Cyrillic, Kazakh Cyrillic, and Azeri Latin (Uzbek Latin uses no characters outside of the English alphabet).

For each language, cross-platform fonts were created using Altsys Fontographer©.[8] The fonts were packaged for Macintosh and Windows into self-extracting archives that install the fonts automatically. In a Windows environment, the user need only download the font to his desktop, double-click the file, and the fonts automatically install. Using a simple, inexpensive software (WinZip Self Extractor[9]) a self extracting archive was created with the "extract to" parameter set to C:\\WINDOWS\FONTS for Windows 95/98 and C:\\WINNT\FONTS for NT, 2000, and ME. The archive also includes a command line option where it instructs Windows Explorer to open the fonts folder. The action of opening a window on the fonts directory forces an API command that refreshes the Windows font registry and sends the updated information to any open programs. Thus, the Web browser is informed of the new fonts and will not require a restart to display the newly added characters. Unfortunately, in a Macintosh environment, the user needs to move the fonts to his System/Fonts directory and restart his browser. Detailed directions have been provided to help the user get the fonts working properly.

DESIGNING AN ARCHITECTURE OF INTERACTIVITY

The final technical challenge was to create a consistent, scalable architecture for the language-learning activities that would be built around the video clips. Technologies considered included self-contained Java applets; database-driven, dynamically rendered Web pages generated with XML, ASP or PHP[10]; and a client-

---

[8] See http://www.macromedia.com/software/fontographer/
[9] See http://www.winzip.com/winzipse.htm
[10] For the sake of simplicity, these technologies can be defined as scripting languages and markup protocols that allow Web pages to be generated dynamically from database-filled templates — allowing content to be simply dumped into a working model.

side[11] combination of JavaScript and Dynamic Hypertext Markup Language (DHTML). JavaScript was eventually chosen as the principal scripting language due to its speed of execution and its ability to provide complex interactivity within the client-side environment of a Web browser. JavaScript's reliance upon browser architecture, however, subjects its execution to the inconsistencies inherent within the various browsers' object and event models. As programming on the CenAsiaNet project commenced, the two leading Web browsers — Microsoft Internet Explorer and Netscape Navigator — had each recently released browsers capable of unprecedented client-side interaction. Regrettably, the technologies that emerged with these browsers are competing and often incompatible. As a result of this divergence of standards, Web developers have been forced to either write multiple versions of their scripts or to write scripts capable of discriminating browser (as well as platform/operating system) inconsistencies.

The CenAsiaNet architecture utilizes JavaScript's inherent ability to "sniff out" the client environment in which it executes. Each script begins by determining whether it is executing in Internet Explorer or Netscape Navigator and whether that browser is on a Macintosh or on a PC. Each client environment has a different set of standards and requires its own idiosyncratic syntax. In order to execute consistently in a wide variety of browser environments, a script, such as that which drives drag-and-drop activities, identifies its environment and sets a number of string variables that will be used to write code that is compliant with the object model of the client browser. In Figure 3, we see that the script begins by determining which type of browser (Internet Explorer or Netscape) it is loading and, if it finds itself in a Netscape environment, next checks the version number. Browser-specific syntax variables are then populated with the appropriate references so that subsequent functions can, in a single statement, satisfy the syntactical rules of multiple object models. To illustrate this point, Figure 3 includes a function from the drag-and-drop script called *getObject()*, which identifies a draggable object when the user clicks on it. The statement, *theObj = eval("document." + range + obj + styleObj)*, returns syntactically distinct object references for Netscape 4, Netscape 6, and Internet Explorer because the values for the variables *range* and *styleObj* were discriminately set as the script initially loaded.

The Web developers for CenAsiaNet aggressively tested each script in CenAsiaNet through a variety of different platforms (Macintosh, PC) and different browsers (Internet Explorer v.3-v.5.5, Netscape Navigator v.4-v.6) to ensure that every operation was carried out flawlessly in every circumstance.

---

[11] An important distinction needs to be made here between client-side and server-side interaction: Client-side interaction refers to interaction that occurs when a script loads completely onto an end user's (client's) machine and all processes and decisions that occur do so on the user's own computer. Conversely, with server-side interactions, data must be sent from the user's machine to the hosting server. The data is the processed and a decision is sent back across the Internet to the user's machine. Obviously, if connectivity is less than optimal, this process can be cumbersome.

```
//instantiate browser id variables-these help determine which browser
  is being used (Internet Explorer or Netscape Navigator)
    var isIE4;
    var isNav4;
    var isNav5;
//instantiate version variable-these help determine which version of
  the browser is being used (Internet Explorer 4.0, 5.0, etc.)
    var appNum parseInt(navigator.appVersion.charAt(0));
    if (appNum > 4) {
        //set IEspecific syntax-if the browser is Internet Explorer, this
          command tells the script to apply all styles related to
          Internet Explorer only.
            if (navigator.appName != "Netscape") {
            isIE4 = true;
            range = "all.";
            styleObj = ".style";
            }
        //set Nav5 specific syntax-if the browser is Netscape Navigator
          6, this command tells the script to apply all styles related to
          Netscape 6 only.
            if (navigator.appName == "Netscape" && appNum < 5) {
            isNav4 = true;
            insideWindowWidth = window.innerWidth;
            range = "";
            styleObj = "";
            }
        //set Nav4 specific syntax-if the browser is anything under
          Netscape Navigator 6, this command tells the script to apply
          all styles related to Netscape 4.7 and under.
            if (navigator.appName == "Netscape" && appNum > 4) {
            isNav5 = true;
            insideWindowWidth = window.innerWidth;
            range = "";
            styleObj = "";
            }
}
//convert object name string or object reference into a valid object
  reference-this command adds additional style requirements depending
  on the browser that is being used.
    function getObject(obj) {
    var theObj;
        if (typeof obj == "string") {
            if (isNav5) {
            theObj = document.getElementById(obj);
            }
            else {
            theObj = eval("document." + range + obj + styleObj);
            }
        }
        else {
        theObj = obj;
        }
return theObj;
}
```

Figure 3. Cross-browser Javascript code
(an excerpt from the drag and drop script)

A directory, or library, of a few core JavaScripts controls the interactivity of the hundreds of language activities that accompany the CenAsiaNet video clips. By residing in a remote library, as opposed to being embedded in the head of each HTML document, a single script can control an infinite number of activities. As a result, the ability for maintaining and enhancing the interaction within the materials has remained extremely high, even as the number of activities has substantially grown.

Another factor that has allowed for rapid growth of the number of activities is a series of templates that has been created for the production of exercises. These templates are HTML documents that reference the remote scripts in the JavaScript library and contain embedded calls to functions within the script. The developer need only pass the content of the language activity to the script and all of the HTML and corresponding scripted interaction is generated automatically.

For example, the script call

```
writeRadio ('Turkmenistan !gaz! ~irana satar', 'nebit',
'pagta');
```

will produce the multiple choice question shown in Figure 4.

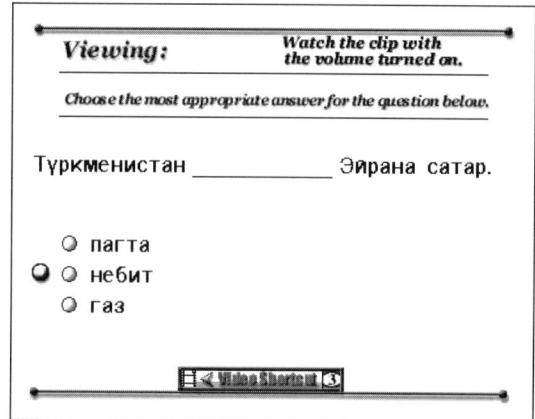

Figure 4. A Turkmen multiple-choice activity

The script looks for the correct answer from the statement in the first argument that is passed to it from the *writeRadio()* call (*Turkmenistan !gaz! ~irana satar*[12]). It interprets the string that is delimited by exclamation marks (gaz) as the correct answer. It then extracts the word for the sentence and randomly shuffles it in with the distracters (nebit and pagta) as possible choices for completing the sentence. When the student selects one of the choices, the script knows whether the choice is

---

[12] The sentence translates to "Turkmenistan sells gas to Iran." The HTML font tags (<FONT FACE='ER UniversTMEN'>) are automatically inserted by the script. When the page loads, the program determines which language is being worked with and pulls the font reference from an array that holds the name of each language and its corresponding font name.

correct or incorrect and responds accordingly. If the answer is correct, immediate judgmental feedback is given by turning the yellow button to the left of the choices green, while a wrong answer elicits a red button. The script also logs the results in a pair of scoring variables *(numRight/numWrong)*.

As JavaScript resides solely on the client's machine, the scores that it records are temporary, unless they are passed to a server-side script that can record the data to a more permanent location. The technical team at the American Councils has built a simple database application to handle the recording of scores on the CenAsiaNet Web server. The PERL application first receives a student's scores as they are passed by JavaScript as values in a hidden form element.[13] The scores are then written to a flat text file and tagged with the login name *($ENV{REMOTE_USER})* that was entered when the student arrived at the site. The scores can later be accessed by the user and e-mailed directly to the instructor if the user is a student who is using the materials as a part of an established course. The teacher also has the option of reviewing students' scores online.

CONCLUSION

Many of the challenges that arose with the CenAsiaNet project were expected — a good deal more unfolded as the work was undertaken. Pedagogically, the greatest challenge came in trying to coordinate with materials developers who are spread around the globe and have little experience designing materials for a CALL environment. The other major difficulty was due to the content of the video itself. By their very nature, Central Asian news broadcasts are dry and visually uninspiring. The CenAsiaNet team hopes to resolve this second issue in the production of subsequent modules by moving away from news broadcasts towards more visually stimulating and culturally rich video content.

On the technical end, several key lessons were learned in terms of video delivery, font issues, scripting interactivity, and instructional design. Regarding video delivery, in cases where the video is only supplementary to other materials, RealPlayer is a satisfactory choice, due to its excellent streaming capabilities. However, when the video is the primary text and focus of an exercise, as in the CenAsiaNet modules, QuickTime has been deemed the better choice. In such a case, the integrity of the original video is of the utmost importance in carrying out the tasks in the lessons, and QuickTime, although a slightly slower download, can better guarantee this integrity in an embedded video format.

One of the strengths of CenAsiaNet is the transparency of its instructional design. The developers knew and understood CenAsiaNet's target audience — language professionals and language students, not technology specialists. Therefore, an

---

[13] For more information on <HIDDEN> form elements and passing data to server-side applications, see:
http://developer.netscape.com/docs/manuals/communicator/jsref/form2.htm#101126

important goal was to take as many technological tasks out of the user's hand as possible. One example of this is the ability to simply download and click on the fonts, without having to configure keyboard drivers or system preferences. The module also takes users step-by-step through the installation and set-up of the QuickTime plug-in and provides detailed online help for working with the activities.

As is usually the case with technology, something created for today's technology often needs to be adaptable to the demands of emerging technologies. For this reason, the use of a core JavaScript library has been essential to ensuring the sustainability of the CenAsiaNet modules. Once a new technology appears, the developers are able to make the changes to ensure compatibility almost immediately: developers do not need to create a new set of templates or rewrite hundreds of different files in order to adapt the modules.

The CenAsiaNet team has created an innovative resource for Internet-based language learning that they hope may serve as a model for further development of language resources for less commonly taught languages.

Alexander Dunkel, Scott Brill, & Bryan Kohl
University of Arizona

THE IMPACT OF SELF-INSTRUCTIONAL TECHNOLOGY ON LANGUAGE LEARNING: A VIEW OF NASILP

The National Association of Self-Instructional Language Programs (NASILP) is North America's oldest professional organization specifically devoted to fostering the study of less commonly taught languages (LCTLs) through self-instructional principles developed for an academic setting. NASILP provides channels through which member organizations share their areas of expertise. It promotes a modified form of self-accessed instruction to be assessed according to the "Prochievement" model, consisting of an oral achievement test in a proficiency modality given in the target language (Dunkel, 2000). A student's performance is evaluated according to the following criteria:

- Grammatical accuracy
- Vocabulary use and pronunciation
- Communicative competence: fluency, comprehension, and cultural appropriateness

Languages offered at various NASILP institutions vary from year to year depending upon demand. NASILP member institutions offer the following 49 languages:

American Sign Language	Hungarian	Romanian
Apache	Indonesian	Russian
Arabic	Irish (Gaelic)	Serbo-Croatian
Armenian	Italian	Siswati
Cambodian (Khmer)	Japanese	Slovak
Cantonese	Kazakh	Slovenian
Czech	Korean	Swahili
Danish	Lao	Swedish
Dutch	Latvian	Tagalog
Finnish	Lithuanian	Telegu
French	Mandarin (Chinese)	Thai
German	Norwegian	Turkish
Greek (Modern)	Persian	Ukrainian
Haitian-Creole	Polish	Urdu
Hebrew	Portuguese (Brazilian)	Vietnamese
Hindi	Quechua	Yoruba
Hmong		

NASILP has over 114 institutional members providing self-managed programs in the above languages to over 9,100 students. Most institutional members are universities (60%) and colleges (33%), although two-year colleges (3%) and

---

Dunkel, A., Brill, S., & Kohl, B. (2002). The impact of self-instructional technology on language learning: A view of NASILP. In C. A. Spreen (Ed.), *New technologies and language learning: Cases in the less commonly taught languages* (Technical Report #25; pp. 97–120). Honolulu, HI: University of Hawai'i, Second Language Teaching & Curriculum Center.

secondary schools (4%) are increasing in membership (all figures courtesy NASILP Secretariat). Institutional membership provides access to the Association's resources and services, especially in the area of curriculum design and instructional methodologies that incorporate a high degree of assessment (quality control) through a network of specialists from universities throughout the United States.

NASILP serves as the only direct national forum for the interchange of ideas and expertise for the development and support of self-instructional academic curricula for low enrollment languages. Any academic institution may apply for membership. Although the National Council of Less Commonly Taught Languages (NCOLCTL) is a growing link between 17 language and regional professional organizations, NASILP's guidelines affect over 114 programs directly via listserve, Web site, and annual conference.

NASILP provides member institutions with

Resources
- List of external examiners
- Recommended course materials
- Multimedia orientation and training materials for students, tutors, examiners, and coordinators
- CD-ROM language courseware

Consultation

NASILP offers consultations on the development of every aspect of self-accessed academic programs for the less commonly taught languages regarding the roles of the
- Student
- Tutor
- Tutorial session
- Examiner
- Coordination
- Guidelines for the standardization of testing procedures and curriculum design and operation

Annual conference and workshop

Members are encouraged to attend an annual 2-day conference and workshop. This conference is equally informative for new as well as long-standing members. It covers topics such as program design, budgeting, implementation of new language offerings, and the responsibilities of students, tutors, coordinators and examiners. It features presentations reflecting current research on issues pertinent to academically based self-accessed programs for LCTLs. The conference also provides access to nationally recognized scholars in the fields of pedagogy, design, materials development, instructional technologies, and program administration, and establishes channels through which the special concerns and expertise of NASILP's institutional members are shared.

NASILP institutional structure

NASILP offers the following benefits to language programs seeking to offer LCTLs:

- It has a wide variety of language offerings, from the less commonly taught LCTLs such as Italian and Japanese to *the least* commonly taught LCTLs such as Apache, Kazakh, Lao, and Romanian.
- Its programs are cost-effective alternatives when it is financially unfeasible to hire full-time faculty for a very low enrollment language.
- Its methods have proven to be an academically sound, rigorous, and a viable alternative to traditional instructor-based language instruction.

NASILP was founded in 1973 to meet the needs of LCTL students at institutions where there were an insufficient number of traditional language classes. From the beginning it was oriented to meet the challenges presented by the distance between available faculty and interested students in institutions scattered throughout the US.

NASILP addresses the limited availability of LCTL faculty by providing member programs with contact information for language examiners throughout the country who agree to examine students according to NASILP guidelines. Accredited examinations provide students a standard by which to assess their language abilities. Honoraria, travel, and per diem are the only examiner-related program expenses. Audio-lingual practice is provided by tutorial sessions, in which a native speaker, engaged locally, meets with students two to three times a week to enhance student mastery of recorded materials studied daily on a student's own time.

NASILP offers a model that is thus much more cost-effective than standard language programs for the teaching of LCTLs. *However, it must be emphasized that NASILP's goal is to enhance and promote LCTL offerings, not to eliminate or replace existing departments and programs.*

New technology endeavors

Since NASILP's founding, technology has been at the center of its operation — the organization was created due to the development of the portable audiocassette tape recorder and the availability of text and tape materials from sources such as the Foreign Service Institute (FSI). The guidelines require that course materials offer practical, authentic language in the form of recorded materials. Cassette tapes have always been the most common media format, but are gradually being replaced by Computer Assisted Language Learning (CALL) materials in the form of CD-ROMs and Internet-delivered courseware. In 1999–2000, CD-ROMs accounted for 14% of

NASILP instructional materials, compared with 1% in 1998–1999 and 0% in 1997–1998. Textbooks with accompanying audiocassettes made up the remaining 86%; 11% of the materials included in the total incorporated both audio and video tapes (NASILP Secretariat).

In the past 4 years, with support from the National Security Education Program (NSEP), NASILP has developed the following four technology projects:

- The *Critical Languages Series*™ of six CD-ROM LCTL courseware sets.
- The *MaxAuthor*™ authoring system, dedicated to the production of language materials for dissemination on CD-ROM and the Internet.
- *LCTL FAQ pages* for Internet delivery, addressing language-specific questions frequently asked by both students and teachers, with special attention given to use of CALL materials.
- *NASILP guidelines* on the Internet for students, tutors, examiners, and coordinators (available to members at www.nasilp.org).

The following sections examine projects and their impact on student learning.

THE CRITICAL LANGUAGES SERIES

Lack of quality materials has been one of the major historic impediments facing language educators mainly because publishers have concentrated on the larger, more commonly taught language markets. The Critical Languages Series (CLS) of CD-ROM courseware for Brazilian Portuguese, Cantonese, Chinese, Kazakh, Korean, and Turkish was completed over a 3-year period. Each classroom-tested, MS-Windows double CD-ROM package contains 20 lessons for the beginning learner comprised of video dialogues and readings by native speakers, thousands of audio recordings, exercises, graphics and extensive cultural and grammatical notes. CLS was created with MaxAuthor, a freely available authoring system (see section below) that has been under development at the University of Arizona (UA) for the past 16 years. CLS was developed using NASILP guidelines, with additional refinements based on input from NASILP members and beta testing with NASILP students.

The CD-ROM format allows for the combination of multiple elements into a single unit — the equivalents of a conventional textbook, workbook, audio, and video. "*Beginning Cantonese* is...user-friendly, linguistically and pedagogically very sound, well conceived, and quite affordable" (Yang, 2001, p.623). The CD-ROM format (as opposed to Internet delivery) also reaches students who do not have access to an Internet connection, especially at home. Over 1000 copies of CLS titles have been sold and are being used by independent learners worldwide. Proceeds from the sales of the Critical Languages Series are funding new NASILP-oriented materials projects, including "Continuing Kazakh" (Level II) and "Beginning Tohono O'odham."

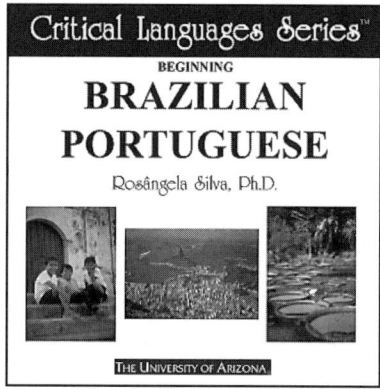

Figure 1. CLS CD-ROM cover

ACCOMMODATING LEARNER STYLES

CLS accommodates different learning styles in an innovative and integrative way. The authors have provided a suggested activity list for each lesson, meant as a guide to optimize student use of their materials. Students are encouraged to adjust the sequence of activities to reflect their own personal learning strategies. However, they are not required to access or adhere to this list, and may choose to pursue the materials independently. Studies have shown that many students respond more positively to learning through aural or visual elements, while others are more comfortable with textual materials (Lepke, 1977). Not only does this provide ample material for these different learning affinities, it integrates them together: text corresponds to audio and video. Text and audio are directly combined in exercises like *Pronunciation, Listening Dictation,* and *Audio Flashcards.* Learners are thus able to study according to their own preferences, but can also easily expand on these by regular use of all the elements of the courseware. This can also serve to keep student interest — a key element of self-instruction. *"Beginning Brazilian Portuguese...* content is rich, organized and up-to-date. It accommodates different learning styles, and allows students to explore Brazilian culture, vocabulary, and grammar in context" (Jouët-Pastré, 2000). CLS is currently being used in three settings: the traditional classroom; a modified self-instructional setting; and completely self-instructional, non-credit contexts.

VIDEO

The cornerstone of CLS lessons is provided by video dialogs. These convey a story line with well-developed characters. Research has supported the use of video in CALL materials:

> The investigation has yielded the conclusion that a video clip is more effective in teaching unknown vocabulary words than a still picture. Among the suggested factors that explain such a result are that video better builds a mental image, better creates curiosity leading to increased concentration, and embodies an advantageous combination of modalities (vivid or dynamic image, sound, and printed text). (Al-Seghayer, 2001, p. 202)

The introduction of video also creates a contextual situation to help develop cultural awareness. For example, in *Beginning Brazilian Portuguese*, a video clip shows conventional hand gestures used by Brazilians to convey concepts that reflect Brazilian cultural mores. Both Cantonese and Chinese give multiple examples of poetry recitations: There are children's poems used in games, adult poems used to convey serious philosophical and literary concepts, and in one case, a Cantonese call-and-response poem done in a playful dramatic style.

The CD-ROM format provides rich multimedia interaction in which is difficult to duplicate on the Internet because of limited or unreliable bandwidth, although this should be possible in the near future.

CRITICAL LANGUAGES SERIES ASSESSMENT

Determining the effectiveness of language learning technology is well known to be a very difficult problem. One major reason for this is that the validity and reliability of instruments measuring student outcomes on language competency are questionable and highly variable (Noijons, 1993). This is especially troublesome for LCTL materials since there are so few students using language technology, resulting in very little quantitative data. We have made a great effort to have each one of the Critical Languages Series reviewed by the major academic journals in the field (Al-Seghayer, 2001; Son, 2000; Sandrelli, 2000; Wells, 2000; Zheng, 2001). These reviews as well as student surveys, comments from users, and emerging academic research on language acquisition, will help shape our future courseware.

Beginning Korean and Turkish language courses at UA used CLS CD-ROMs as primary "texts" for the 2000–2001 academic year. Students were given a full demonstration of the features of the CD-ROMs at the beginning of the academic year. They were instructed to use the CD-ROMs daily for at least an hour outside of class. In doing so, they were expected to familiarize themselves with the content of the lesson texts, to use the exercises and multimedia components to improve their knowledge of vocabulary and grammatical structure, and to sharpen their skills in pronunciation and listening comprehension. Twice a week, they met for an hour in small groups with native-speaking tutors in the target language. Utilizing printouts of the lesson texts from the CD-ROMs, tutors reviewed subject topics and linguistic features presented in each lesson by means of role-playing exercises and lesson dialogs.

The CLS courseware development team prepared a questionnaire to be answered anonymously by these students in order to elicit their opinions regarding use of integrated multimedia and hyper-textual materials as primary course "texts," and in order to indicate patterns of use for these materials. The questionnaires were attached to a UA/ Critical Languages Program (CLP) course evaluation form given to each student as s/he emerged from the individually administered oral final examination at the conclusion of the 2001 spring semester. Twenty-four Turkish students and eight Korean students filled out the questionnaire, providing a sample of 32. Details of this survey are shown in Figures 2 through 8.

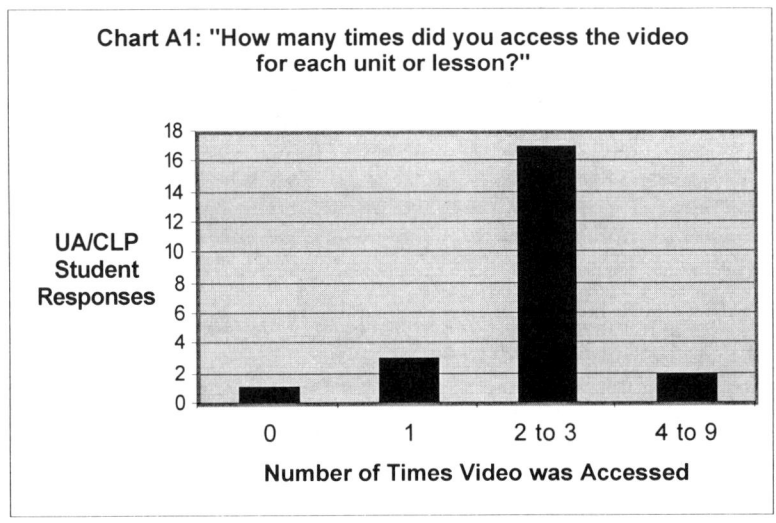

Figure 2. In response to the question
"How many times did you access the video for each unit or lesson?"

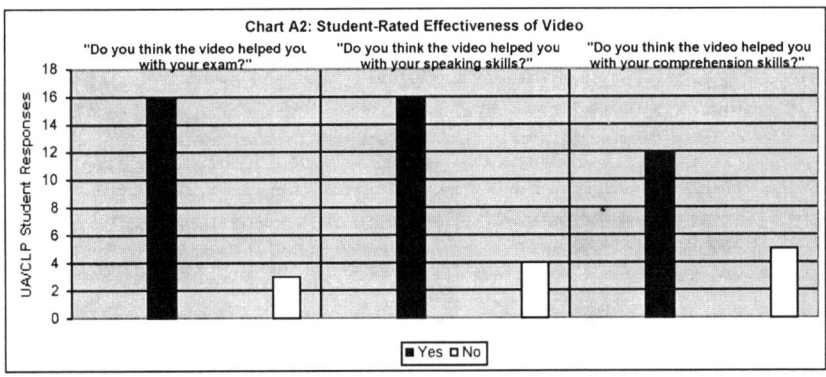

Figure 3. Student-rated effectiveness of video

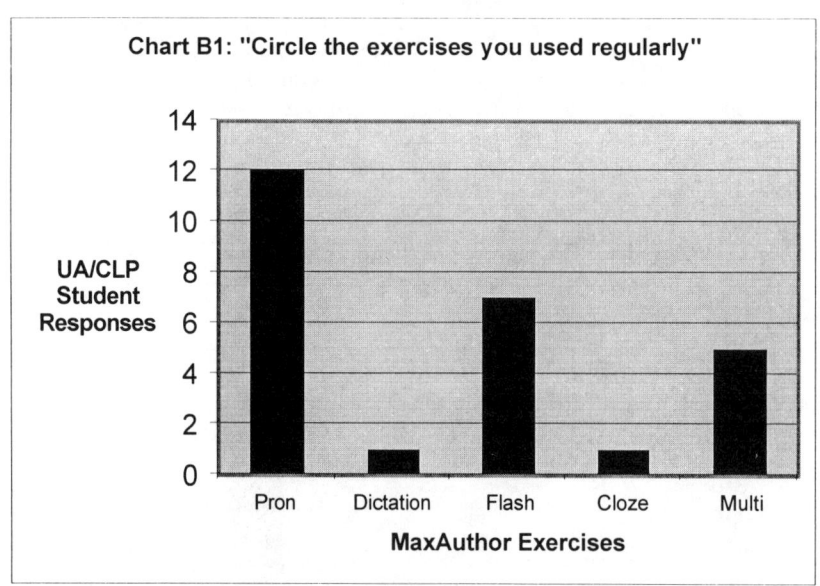

Figure 4. In response to the instruction
"Circle the exercises you used regularly."

Please see Appendix A: MaxAuthor Exercise Formats for descriptions of each exercise activity.

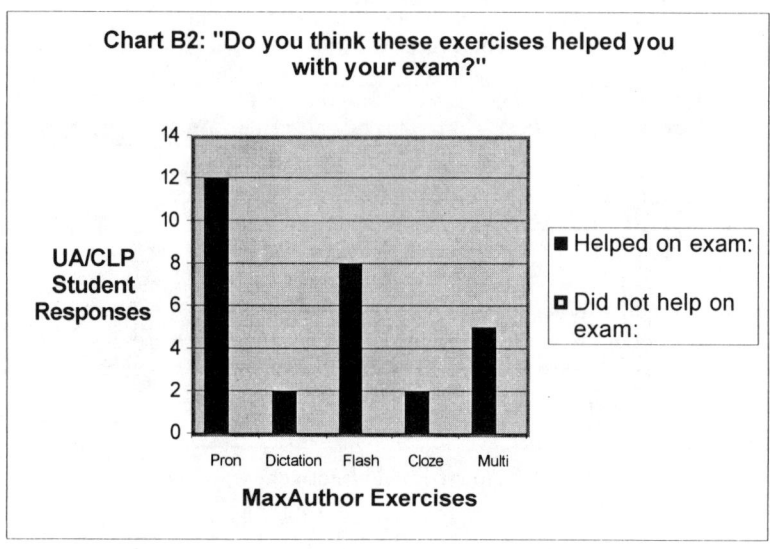

Figure 5. In response to the question
"Do you think these exercises helped you with your exam?"

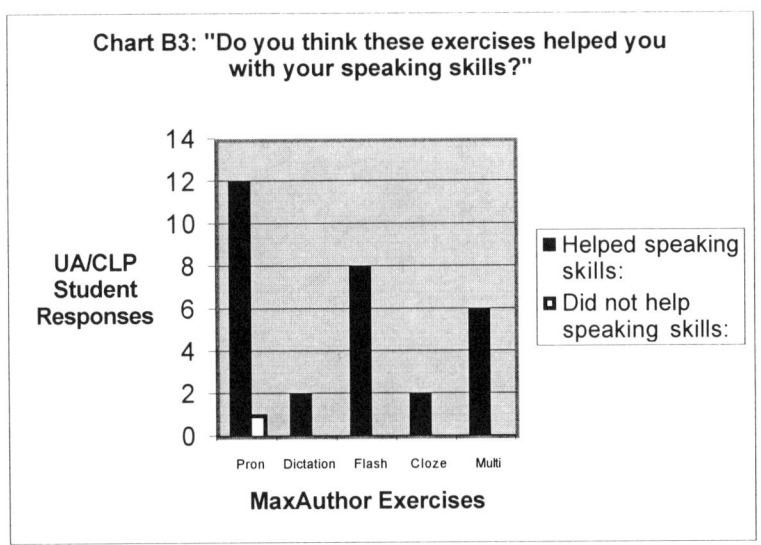

Figure 6. In response to the question
"Do you think these exercises helped you with your speaking skills?"

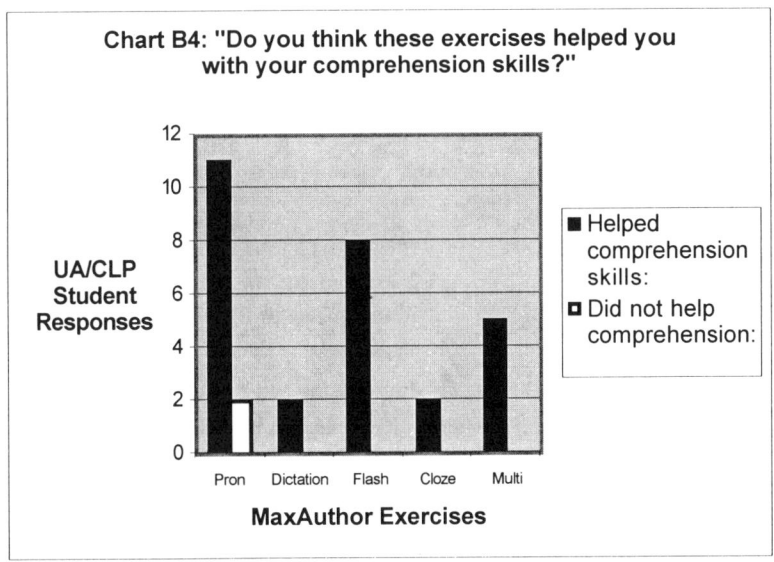

Figure 7. In response to the question
"Do you think these exercises helped you with your comprehension skills?"

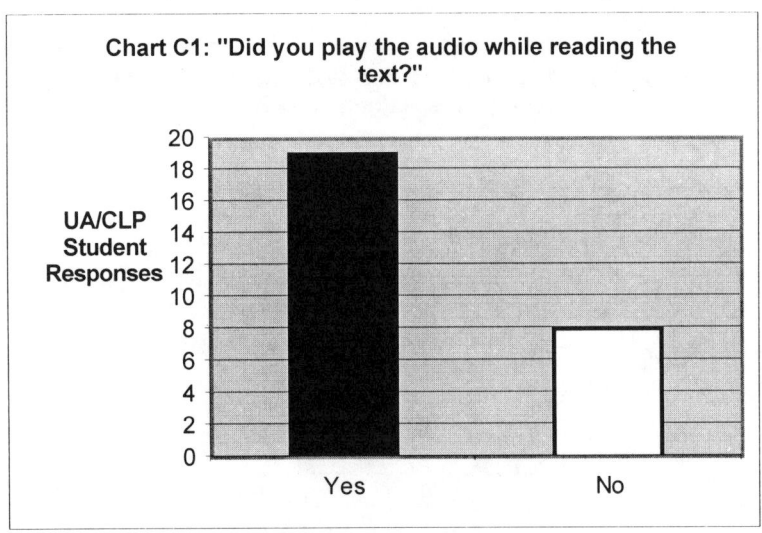

Figure 8. In response to the question
"Did you play the audio while reading the text?"

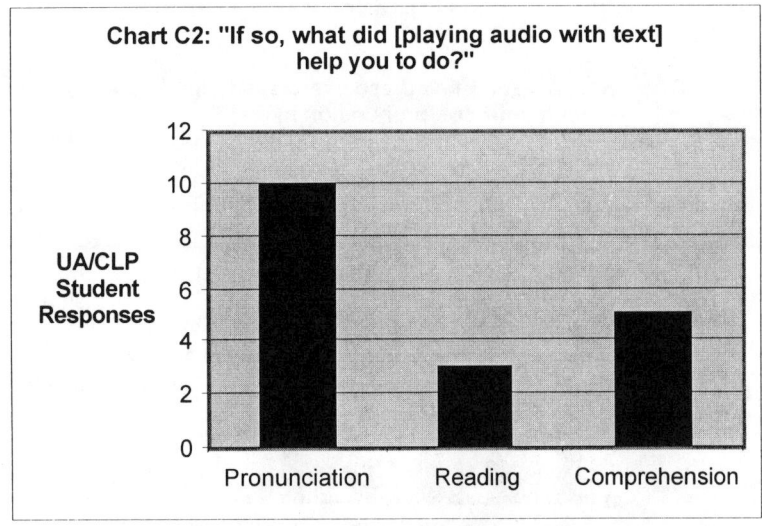

Figure 9. In response to the question
"If so, what did [playing the audio with the text] help you to do?"

One of the more notable findings resulting from the questionnaire is that the students reported that the CD-ROMs' exercises, particularly *Pronunciation* and *Audio Flashcards*, helped them prepare for examinations, and improved their speaking and comprehension skills (Figure 5, 6, and 7). Video was also shown to be helpful for these purposes (Figure 3). Students reported that they did not access the word and sentence audio recordings while reading the lesson texts proper as regularly as they did the video (Figures 2 and 8). However, the central role played by word and sentence audio recordings in *Pronunciation, Listening Dictation,* and *Audio Flashcards* exercises demonstrates their usefulness as applied to other contexts. Finally, the indications that *Listening Dictation* and *Vocabulary Completion* were not used as often as other courseware features identify these as subjects demanding further research — in assessment of our current products as well as toward future courseware development.

Although these are subjective assessments given at a single point in time, the context in which they were given is a critical and revealing one. Because they were volunteered by students immediately after completion of the final examination, before final grades had been given, they reflect each student's self-assessment of her or his own language capabilities, as *directly related* to their use of CLS CD-ROMs to gain these capabilities. Although this context does not ensure greater accuracy of assessment, it provides a valuable view of individual patterns of use and personal feedback given independent of institutional accreditation. The CLS courseware development team is currently preparing a formal, long-term research design to further assess its accomplishments.

MAXAUTHOR: A FREE MULTIMEDIA AUTHORING SYSTEM FOR LANGUAGE INSTRUCTION

The University of Arizona's Computer Aided Language Instruction Group (CALI) has made its MS-Windows and Internet-based multimedia CALL authoring system freely available for non-commercial use (http://cali.arizona.edu/docs/wmaxa). MaxAuthor has been under development for 16 years and was used by authors nationwide to create the Critical Languages Series of language instructional CD-ROMs. After a two-hour tutorial, MaxAuthor enables teachers with only word-processing computer skills to create interactive exercises and multimedia instructional materials for 22 languages, including Cantonese, Chinese (with optional Pinyin), Dutch, English, French, German, Italian, Japanese, Kazakh, Korean, Lummi, Mojave, Navajo, O'odham, Pinyin Romanization (Mandarin), Portuguese, Russian, Southern Paiute, Spanish, Swedish, Turkish, and Yaqui. Additional languages are under development. Completed courseware can utilize audio, video, footnotes, and graphics. Student activities include MaxBrowser, Listening Dictation, Pronunciation, Multiple Choice, Vocabulary Completion, and Audio Flashcards. Lessons can be delivered via Internet or MS-Windows. Improvements are continually being made to the software.

The author records separate audio for both sentences and words and has the option of recording audio in the training language only, but can also record translations or paraphrases in up to five other languages or dialects. The author can either manually define the word and sentence boundaries or let MaxAuthor choose the boundaries automatically.

MaxAuthor works just like a text editor with tools that add audio and exercise material; there is no programming or scripting necessary. The author selects one of the five authoring views: Word, Sentence, Multiple Choice, Footnote, or Cloze (Vocabulary Completion). The tools within MaxAuthor let you play, record, or edit recordings. When the *Record All* menu choice is selected, MaxAuthor sequentially records each word or sentence. When a lesson text is comprised of multiple occurrences of the same word, there is an option of using the same recording for each occurrence to avoid re-recording the same word.

Once audio has been recorded for the lesson, the student can immediately use *MaxBrowser, Listening Dictation, Pronunciation, Multiple Choice, Vocabulary Completion,* and *Audio Flashcards* without further customization. By adding more information to the lesson such as multiple choice questions, multimedia footnotes, and custom Vocabulary Completion blanks, the richness of the student's interaction with the lesson can be further enhanced. It is the instructor's choice to decide how much time to invest in the lessons.[1] There are approximately 150 registered users of MaxAuthor worldwide.

To this end, language instructors designed MaxAuthor from its inception for ease of use. As Dr. Dana Bourgerie, Head of the Chinese Section, Brigham Young University states

> Anyone with moderate, general computing skills should be able to author lessons in a short time. Indeed, after giving an hour introduction to my research assistant, she was able to create basic MAX lessons. I began authoring lessons after a short orientation session. I find the hyper linking feature easy to use and convenient in providing graphics and notes. I have found the program to be very stable. (D. S. Bourgerie, personal communication, March 28, 2000)

CHALLENGES OF DELIVERING LCTL MATERIALS ON THE INTENET

Even though the Web is worldwide, most Internet browsers have difficulty displaying many of the world's most common languages. Fortunately, this situation is improving. MaxAuthor can deliver online language lessons in all of the 23 languages supported; see http://cali.arizona.edu/maxnet for examples. For Cantonese, Kazakh, Navajo, and O'odham, custom embedded fonts are used due to the lack of browser support.

NASILP GUIDELINES ON THE INTERNET

Since November 2000, NASILP has been using the Internet to disseminate guidelines for students, tutors, examiners, and coordinators. RealServer ™ is being used using to stream (transmit) materials that were previously only available on

---

[1] MaxAuthor workshops have been presented at the following conferences: CALICO 2000, 2001, NECTFL 2001, and IALL 2001. There are approximately 150 registered users of MaxAuthor worldwide.

videotape mailed by a central distribution point. Digital delivery of these guidelines provides an added benefit: The transcripts of the guidelines can be searched by keyword so that topics of interest can be accessed without "rewinding" or "fast forwarding" an entire videotape. These materials were designed with the parallel intent to encourage users (especially new NASILP members) to become familiar and comfortable with multimedia-based learning methods and the concept of learner-directed instruction.

A freely accessible Web page, http://clp.arizona.edu/nasilp/sample.htm, enables students to see and hear NASILP's Distinguished Director, Eleanor Jordan, and Executive Director Emeritus, John Means, answer questions about NASILP and help students understand their role in a modified self-instructional language program. It also shows prospective member institutions the kind of materials available if they join NASILP. This and other interactive informational resources are available to current members in the password-protected "Members Only" region of the NASILP Web site.

LCTL FAQ PAGES ON THE INTERNET

NASILP is facilitating pedagogical support for LCTLs through the Internet. It is expanding its Web site to include detailed, hyperlinked reference pages addressing language-specific questions frequently asked by both students and teachers, with special attention given to use of CALL materials. Currently, reference pages have been completed for seven LCTLs, including Brazilian Portuguese, Chinese, Czech, Japanese, Korean, Polish, and Ukrainian. Twelve additional languages including Arabic, Cantonese, Hindi/Urdu, Hungarian, Kazakh, Persian, Rumanian, Russian, Serbo-Croatian, Thai, Turkish, and Vietnamese are in the planning stage. Each LCTL will be represented by a unique set of resources, developed by a designated expert for each language.

The infrastructure of NASILP will continue to grow and be strengthened through a comprehensive professional development and recruitment effort that involves greater use of Web pages and links to assess and remedy needs in the LCTL teaching and learning community. The growing electronic network linking several institutions and programs will further strengthen other institutional networks and linkages nationwide, a primary NSEP goal.

DISCUSSION: CURRENT INSTRUCTIONAL TECHNOLOGIES

The following is in response to questions posed by NSEP for the present study.

Having illustrated the organization of NASILP and discussed the recent technology projects undertaken, specific research questions can now be addressed by summarizing the integration of its existing infrastructure with its technological projects.

USERS

NASILP utilizes technologically based self-instructional materials, including Computer Assisted Language Learning (CALL) course materials. CD-ROM CALL technology has been enthusiastically accepted by users and program administrators, and is expected to replace cassette and videotapes as high-quality courseware becomes more readily available. NASILP directors have also expressed interest in the delivery of CALL materials on the Internet.

NASILP has found that the use of CD-ROMs can significantly reduce student costs provided that they have been designed as a complete course, as is the case with the Critical Languages Series (see above). This, combined with NASILP's established method of sharing institutional resources, addresses issues of both equity and diversity by bringing more languages, even those least commonly taught, within the reach of a broader range of students and institutions. The CD-ROM format is self-contained, which allows students to study on their own time.

The Critical Languages Program at the University of Arizona (CLP) provides an example of how institutional guidelines may be combined with emerging technologies to improve availability, quality, and sustainability of LCTL instruction. CLP courses are established according to student demand, and consist of four to seven students. Media-enhanced course materials allow students daily exposure to spoken language at any time. Audio-lingual practice of these materials is provided by tutorial sessions.

The following factors contribute to low attrition rates at UA: (a) courses are established according to student demand; (b) they are supported by a supplementary fee paid by each student; and (c) all students are instructed on self-motivated learning policy regarding student responsibilities, and are required to sign a memorandum of acceptance before beginning a course.

USES

Our guidelines require that course materials offer practical, authentic language in the form of recorded materials. Materials should be structured in order of increasing linguistic complexity. Content should be presented in order of decreasing commonality of everyday use. Attention should be given to the behavioral culture of societies that use a given language. If both written and spoken elements are to be covered in a course, spoken language should be introduced before written language, and stylistic differences between the two should be stressed. All materials presented in the text for a given course should be addressed in its accompanying recorded media. Recordings should be of native speakers, and should represent conversational language in authentic context.

The Critical Languages Series (CLS) was created with MaxAuthor by a consortium of linguists and computer programmers. MaxAuthor allows authors a format in which non-language technologies, such as hypertext, digital audio and video, and database technology, can be directly applied within lesson texts to language-based technologies such as syntactic categorization, vocabulary extraction, parsing, and text generation.

RESOURCES

Because examiners in LCTLs are not commonly available, NASILP provides contacts with language instructors from the entire United States who agree to give examinations for a given program according to NASILP's "prochievement" model. Honoraria, travel, and per diem are the only examiner-related program expenses. It is not uncommon for one examiner to be affiliated with more than one program.

Student audio-lingual practice is provided two to three times a week in tutorial sessions with a native speaker, engaged locally by a program. Because the native speakers are tutors and not teachers — and thus do not choose materials, set pacing, explain grammar, or give exams or grades — they are not as costly as full-time instructors but are active collaborators in consulting with the examiner to create realizable guidelines.

Our own experience on the UA campus provides a positive example of a self-instructional program as an asset to its host institution despite low enrollments. The CLP works as an instructionally self-sustaining program, in which language sections of four to seven students are established according to student demand, and supported by a supplementary fee paid by each student. This fee covers support services, and native-speaking tutor wages and examiner honoraria. Students are required to purchase their own course materials. Course establishment by student demand reduces attrition rates (7% in 2000–2001), as does the supplementary fee. Small sections allow greater opportunity for applied specialization in content. The Turkish courses are so overwhelmingly attended by engineering students that much of the course's content is now related to engineering. CLP also has its own facilities for courseware production, which have been assisted by NSEP funding, and sustained through returns from commercially published courseware. Thus, at little cost to the university, it generates competency in 14 LCTLs, hosts visiting scholars and professional delegations, and produces critically acclaimed, state-of-the-art language courseware that is now used at institutions throughout the country and abroad.

MaxAuthor enables teachers with only word-processing computer skills to create interactive exercises and multimedia instructional materials for 18 LCTLs, plus English, French, Spanish, and German. After a two-hour self-instructional tutorial, teachers are able to produce materials that can be tailored to their specific instructional needs and contexts — from supplementary exercises at the introductory level to specific sustainment training tasks at Level II and above.

BENCHMARKS

NASILP achievements are summarized below according to the following benchmarks, defined by the Institute for Higher Education Policy (2000):

- *Institutional support: infrastructure issues, technology plan.* NASILP's status as a national organization with nearly 30 years experience, and its membership of over 114 institutions, provides an important infrastructure network for LCTL teachers. It was founded on and is dedicated to the principle of technologically based course materials utilizing a prochievement examination modality. NASILP is also active in maintaining professional ties with other national organizations such as the National Conference on Less Commonly Taught Languages (NCOLCTL).
- *Course development: design, delivery, technology used.* The limited availability of LCTL teachers makes the self-instructional format imperative for the dissemination of LCTL learning. CALL's hyperlinked multimedia/text approach allows author-directed and student-directed learning patterns to converge and collaborate.
- *Teaching/learning: pedagogy, student interaction with faculty, feedback to students.* Current research is highlighting the pedagogical strength of CALL in engaging students and providing them with unlimited access to new vocabulary, native pronunciation, and typical speech patterns.
  NASILP's learner-directed approach provides feedback for students through the tutorial sessions with native speakers, who allow regular speech practice and thus greater familiarity with the spoken language. This improves pronunciation, comprehension, and speech generation ("thinking through the language"). The presence of accredited examinations provides incentive for students to keep up with the course, and gives them a standard by which to assess their language abilities.
- *Course structure: course objectives, library resources, student expectations.* UA/CLP provides an example of how NASILP programs can be self-instructionally sustaining. Courses are established according to student demand and are supported by a supplementary fee paid by each student. This fee covers support services, tutor wages, and examiner fees. Students are required to purchase their own course materials. Course establishment by student demand reduces attrition rates, as does the supplementary fee. Small sections allow for greater opportunity for applied specialization in content.
- *Student support: admissions, financial aid.* Expenses related to the use of multimedia materials have been significantly reduced at UA/CLP through use of CALL materials. CD-ROM-based materials such as the Critical Languages Series allow multiple elements — the equivalents of a conventional textbook, workbook, audio, and video — to be combined into a single unit, the cost of which is typically less than the sum total cost of conventional components. The impending development of Web-based materials will significantly reduce the duplication and distribution costs demanded by CD-ROM production.

- *Faculty support: assist in transition from classroom teaching to online instruction.* After a 2-hour tutorial, MaxAuthor enables teachers with only word-processing computer skills to create interactive exercises and multimedia instructional materials for 18 LCTLs (others are under development) that can be tailored to their specific instructional needs and contexts — from supplementary exercises at the introductory level to specific sustainment training tasks at Level II and above. Instructor access to multimedia equipment — from a simple scanner to a video camera — allows for a variety of authentic linguistic and visual materials to serve as the basis for instructional activities and exercises.

CONCLUSION

Since 1973, NASILP has served as the largest and oldest national forum for the interchange of ideas and expertise toward the development and support of self-instructional academic curricula for LCTLs. NASILP's 114+ member institutions communicate via listserve, Web site, and an annual conference. These member institutions (universities, colleges, and high schools) help over 9,100 students learn nearly fifty LCTLs nationwide. With NSEP funding, NASILP has collaborated with the University of Arizona's Critical Languages Program (CLP) and Computer Aided Language Instruction (CALI) group to a) improve the delivery of information facilitating the administration of member LCTL programs; b) create critically needed, original multimedia language instruction materials based on NASILP guidelines; and c) provide a freely available authoring tool that instructors can use to create their own multimedia language materials.

NASILP's institutional network facilitates assessment of its achievements in CALL. Use of these CD-ROMs has reduced student costs (all courseware components, including text, exercises and media, are contained in one package) and allowed students to use courseware components in an interactive, integrated format on their own schedule. Student surveys show that the CLS CD-ROMs were particularly helpful in preparing for examinations and for improving speaking and comprehension skills.

The support of a national organization such as NASILP has had impact on decisions made by institutions throughout the United States to provide instruction in LCTLs. The successful technology projects discussed here will continue to greatly enhance NASILP's guidance and assessment of LCTL instruction in the years to come, and therefore increase learners' opportunities to study and master these sometimes neglected but strategically important languages.

REFERENCES

Al-Seghayer, K. (2001). The effect of multimedia annotation modes on L2 vocabulary acquisition: A Comparative Study. *Language Learning & Technology,*

5(1), 202–232. Retrieved August 16, 2001, from: http://llt.msu.edu/vol5num1/alseghayer/default.html

Dunkel, A. (2000). Current developments in Less Commonly Taught Languages: A collaborative project. *ADFL Bulletin, 31*(3), 70–72.

Institute for Higher Education Policy. (2000). *Quality on the line: Benchmarks for success in Internet-based distance education.* Washington, DC: National Education Association. Retrieved August 16, 2001, from: http://www.ihep.com/quality.pdf

Jouët-Pastré, C. (2000). [Review of *Beginning Brazilian Portuguese*]. Retrieved August 16, 2001, from University of Hull, C&IT Centre Retrieved August 16, 2001, from: http://www.hull.ac.uk/cti/resources/reviews/begbrazport.htm

Lepke, H. (1977). Discovering student learning styles through cognitive style mapping. In R. Schulz (Ed.), *Personalizing foreign language instruction: Learning styles and teacher options* (pp. 15–20). Skokie, IL: National Textbook Co.

Noijons, J. (1993). Is that what you wanted tested? Testing computer aided language testing (CALT). In F. L. Borchardt & E. Johnson (Eds.), *Proceedings of the 1993 annual symposium: Assessment* (pp. 120–124). Durham, NC: CALICO.

Son, J. (2000). [Review of *Beginning and Continuing Korean*]. Retrieved August 16, 2001, from CALICO Web site: http://astro.temple.edu/~jburston/CALICO/review/critkorean00.htm

Sandrelli, A. (2000). [Review of *Beginning Turkish*]. Retrieved August 16, 2001, from University of Hull, C&IT Centre Retrieved August 16, 2001, from: http://www.hull.ac.uk/cti/resources/reviews/begturk.htm

Wells, P. (2000). [Review of *Beginning Chinese*]. Retrieved August 16, 2001, from University of Hull, C&IT Centre. Retrieved August 16, 2001, from: http://www.hull.ac.uk/cti/resources/reviews/begchin.htm

Yang, P. (2001). [Review of *Beginning Cantonese*]. *CALICO Journal, 18,* 618–628. Retrieved August 16, 2001, from: http://astro.temple.edu/~jburston/CALICO/review/critcantonese00.htm

Zheng, T. (2001). [Review of *Beginning Chinese*]. *CALICO Journal, 18,* 629–639.

APPENDIX: THE MAX FAMILY OF STUDENT APPLICATIONS

MAXBROWSER:
A HYPERTEXT MULTIMEDIA BROWSER FOR LANGUAGE INSTRUCTION

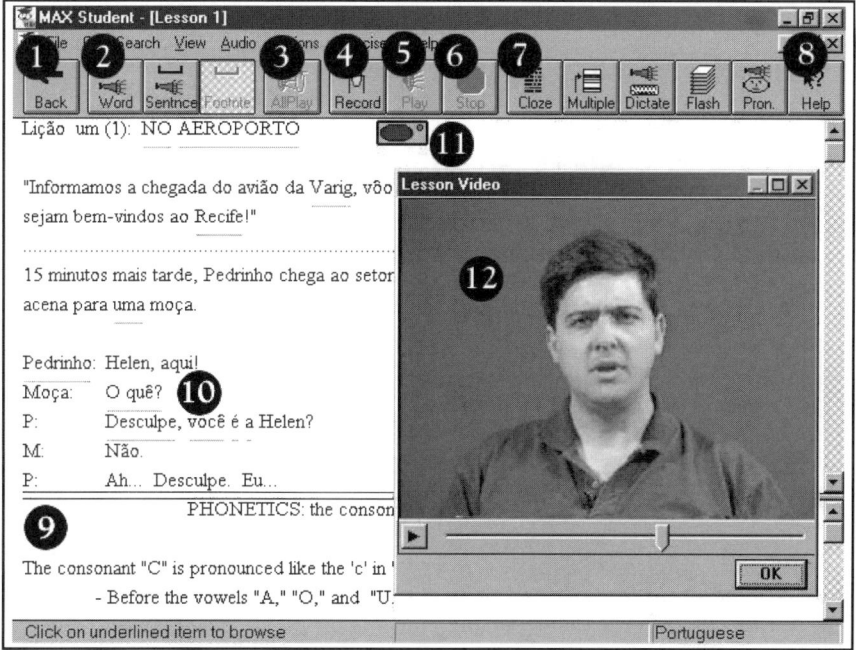

MaxBrowser lets you

- Browse through text with grammatical or cultural footnotes attached. Some footnotes may lead to other lessons, graphics, video.
- Listen to native pronunciations of words and sentences.
- Record your own voice and compare to the native pronunciation.
- Gain further insight into the material by the completion of exercises.

The menu buttons *Word* and *Sent* select either the words or the sentences of the lesson to play. MAX treats lesson text as a collection of words and sentences. There are separate audio recordings for both sentences and words to let you hear the contextual differences between words spoken in isolation and words spoken in sentential context. You can press *W* or *S* to quickly switch between *Word* and *Sent*.

❶ Like the *Back* button in an Internet browser, it allows return to previous page.

❷ Three views of text: *Word, Sentence,* and *Footnote* (here *Word* view is selected). When underlined word or phrase is clicked, hear the native speaker.

❸ Click to *Play All* segments (word or sentence) starting from current position.

❹ *Record* your own voice. Recording continues until *Stop* button is clicked.

❺ After recording your voice in word or sentence, click to play back; then compare your voice with native speaker's.

❻ *Stop* any audio, such as *Play All* or *Record.*

❼ Try one of five available exercises to test and improve your knowledge of the lesson:

Cloze: (fill-in-the-blank) click on blank and type in your answer

Multiple: multiple choice

Dictate: play sentences from lesson; type what you hear

Flash: audio-based flashcard

Pron: helps with pronunciation by playing each word or sentence, then recording your voice to compare with the native speaker's

When you are finished with an exercise, you are returned to MAX.

❽ *Help* explains button or menu function.

❾ *Footnote* window. Drag separator bar up or down to resize footnote window.

❿ A *Word* or *Sentence* that you can click on to hear spoken. Click left mouse button to hear the native language and right mouse button to hear English translation (where available).

⓫ *Video Footnote Indicator.* The icon indicates attached video *Footnote.* Green underlines or icons indicate attached footnote. Either click on icon or switch to

⓬ *Footnote* window for easier access. Footnotes may be textual, graphic, audio, or video, or may access another lesson (a hyperlink).

AUDIO FLASHCARD EXERCISE

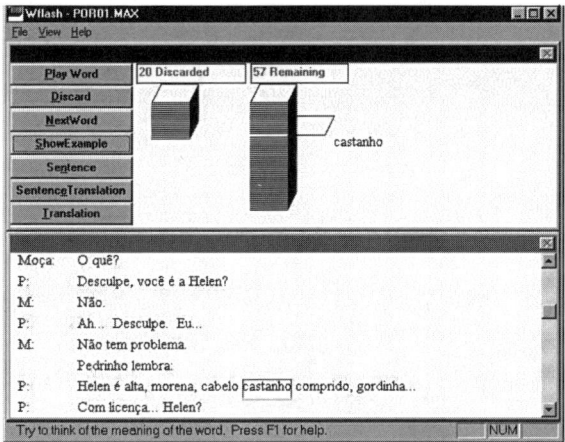

For each lesson, this self-evaluative exercise helps you improve your vocabulary by displaying a deck of visual/aural flash cards. These words are taken directly from the lesson text you have been studying. As each word from the lesson is shown and played, your task is to try to remember of the meaning of the word. When you feel you know the word well enough, the flashcard can be "discarded" so the word will not appear again. The *Remaining* and *Discarded* decks are shown graphically, giving you a feel for your progress.

When a word appears for which you do not know the meaning, you can use some of the clues provided to jog your memory:

- *ShowExample:* shows you an example of the word used in context
- *Sentence:* plays the sentence that the word is a part of
- *Sentence Translation:* plays the translation of the sentence of which the word is part
- Translation: when you give up, plays the translation of the current word

LISTENING DICTATION EXERCISE

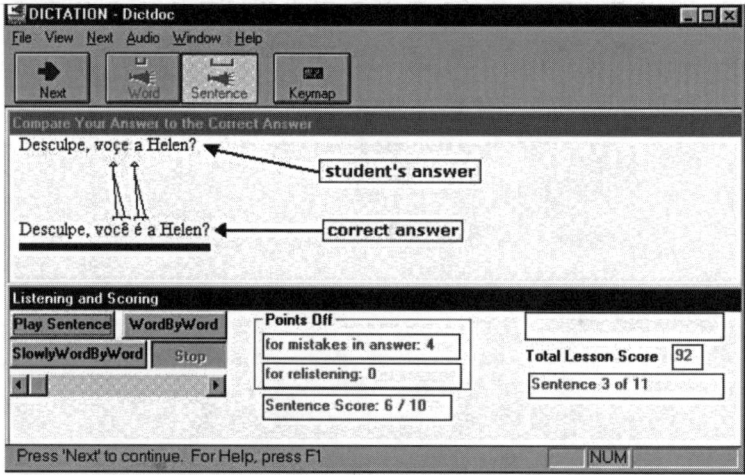

For each lesson, the instructor designates sentences for you to listen to and then type in what you hear. A score is kept to let you know how well you are doing, and you are given immediate feedback on the correctness of your answer with marks that show where mistakes were made. While trying to complete the sentence, you can re-listen to it or listen to it "word by word" or "slowly word by word."

You can also print out a transcription of your answers which can be given to your instructor to show your progress.

MULTIPLE CHOICE EXERCISE

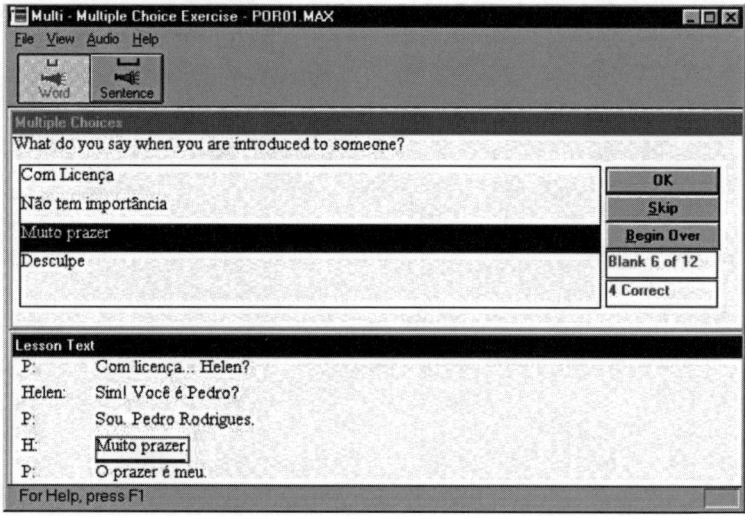

For each lesson, the multiple choice exercise asks questions about a target word or phrase in the lesson text you have been studying. A score is kept to let you know how well you are doing. Simply double click on a choice, and you are given immediate feedback on the correctness of your answer.

Once you have completed all of the multiple choice questions, you are given an opportunity to try again to correctly answer the questions you missed. This process continues until you get them all correct. You can always click on a word or sentence to hear it spoken.

When you have answered the last multiple choice question correctly, you can repeat the exercise by clicking on *Begin Over*, or quit the exercise. You can also print out a transcription of your answers which can be given to your instructor to show your progress.

VOCABULARY COMPLETION (CLOZE) EXERCISE

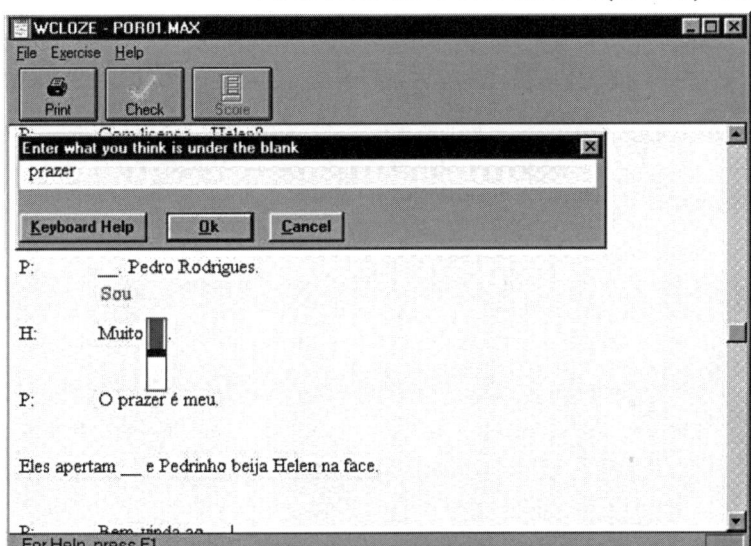

For each lesson, the vocabulary completion (also called Cloze) exercise asks you to fill in the blanks. The blanks may be words or simply a few characters. For some blanks, the student types in an answer and for others, the student selects from a list of choices. When you are finished filling in the blanks, you are shown the correct answers along with your score.

Cloze test performance has proven to be a reliable measure of language ability, which has led to its acceptance in language proficiency certification. The value of the Cloze exercise is that the student must use the context of the entire passage to make the correct selections. The text that you are working with is exactly the same lesson text you've seen before in MaxBrowser, Multiple Choice, Dictation, Pronunciation, and Flashcards. Your previous experience with the text provides additional clues in filling in the blanks. You can print out a transcription of your answers which can be given to your instructor to show your progress.

PRONUNCIATION EXERCISE

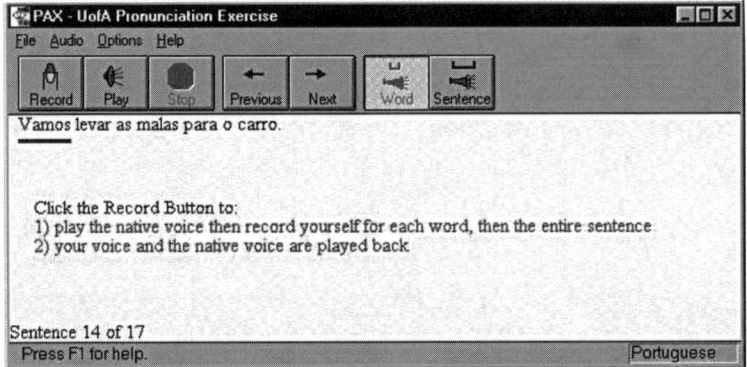

The pronunciation exercise is designed to help students improve pronunciation of words and sentences. This exercise mimics one of the techniques instructors commonly use to improve a student's pronunciation. It first plays the native speaker's voice, and then prompts you to say the same thing (while the appropriate text is being highlighted). You record each word sequentially, and then the whole sentence. After the recordings are completed, the native speaker's voice and the student's voice are played "back-to-back" so the student can compare them. You do not have to press any keys during this process, as the length of the native speaker's recording automatically determines the length of recording for each word.

The text that you are working with is exactly the same lesson text you've seen before in MaxBrowser, Multiple Choice, Dictation, Vocabulary Completion, and Flashcards.

Elizabeth H. D. Mazzocco
University of Massachusetts, Amherst

LANGMEDIA, A WORLD WIDE WEB SITE FOR LANGUAGE AND CULTURE, AND THE ROLE OF INTERNATIONAL STUDENTS IN ITS CREATION

The Five College Foreign Language Resource Center (FCFLRC) received NSEP funding, for a period of 2 years beginning January 1999, to design a Web site that would realize a new, easily accessed Web-based resource for foreign language and cultural studies, LangMedia. The final results of this project can be viewed at http://langmedia.fivecolleges.edu. The offices of Five Colleges, Incorporated (the consortium of Amherst College, Hampshire College, Mount Holyoke College, Smith College, and the University of Massachusetts at Amherst) administered the NSEP grant for our Center. I served as project director and Amy Wordelmn, PhD, the Center's Technology Coordinator, designed the site. This paper will examine the impetus for the site, the decisions that went into its design, and the integral role played by international students in the overall construction of LangMedia.

The finished LangMedia site is more extensive than we had originally planned. Initially, the Web site was to have offered only video (hence our original titling of the site as a video archive), but as our designing proceeded, we decided to add both an audio component and a component of video frames and scanned material to complement the video. LangMedia focuses on some of the least commonly taught languages: Arabic, Bulgarian, Brazilian Portuguese, Croatian, Czech, Hindi, Hungarian, Indonesian, Japanese, Korean, Romanian, Swahili, Thai, Turkish, and Urdu. We anticipated that the Archive would impact all levels of education from middle school through university as well as provide valuable information for the private sector traveling to any destination covered on the Web site. Preliminary results support our suppositions. On the educational side, the site has been accessed by students as young as elementary school, and we have received unsolicited feedback from around the world.

When we began to create the framework of this project 3 years ago, we were inspired by several factors:

- the paucity of all genre of materials readily available to the average person interested in a language or culture that was not considered mainstream, in other words, anything other than Spanish, Italian, French or German;

Mazzocco, E. H. D. (2002). LangMedia, a World Wide Web site for language and culture, and the role of international students in its creation. In C. A. Spreen (Ed.), *New technologies and language learning: Cases in the less commonly taught languages* (Technical Report #25; pp. 121–134). Honolulu, HI: University of Hawai'i, Second Language Teaching & Curriculum Center.

- the significant number of Five College students clamoring for the opportunity to do academic or post-graduate work in a field that required one of the least commonly taught languages; and
- the interest of the government in having materials developed and distributed at low cost to government agencies, the military, and international businesspeople, as well as to institutions of higher learning.

We conceived of LangMedia as an answer to these multiple needs. Because of our day-to-day interaction with language materials, we were (and continue to be) convinced that the future of materials development lay in utilization of the World Wide Web. By exploiting the possibilities for global distribution that the WWW affords us, we felt that we were guaranteed to reach the maximum number of individuals with minimal cost (both to those seeking information and to those paying for creation and distribution of the product).

We also wanted our Web site to serve two distinct groups of people: Those with no prior contact with the target language and its culture, and students of that language and culture. In order to achieve that balance within the project (a balance of both English and the target language), we decided to design each Web page to be user-friendly to any type of individual. Users can click around with ease going from a video clip in the target language, to a target-language transcript of the video, to an English translation of the transcript. The audio phrases are simple and represent target-language phrases that a visitor would need in order to function in a particular country. We also decided to include still images showing the potential traveler such things as a phonecard, a bus ticket, or a hotel bill. In order to bring all the resource material together in an organized way, we chose to begin each page with a paragraph in English. In the end, it was this variety of available sources that caused us to change the name of the Archive to the Media Archive instead of the narrower Video Archive (as originally conceived).

One of the guiding principals in our project development was to present authentic language in its original form. We purposefully did not create any language ourselves in the target language. Therefore, the paragraphs of explanation at the beginning of each page are in English. I strongly believe in the usage of only authentic language for projects such as this one. If an individual wants to learn how to conjugate a verb, s/he can consult a grammar. But if the goal is to listen to a particular language as it is used in daily communication, then an individual can consult our site. I wanted our site to reflect the languages and cultures in their true, unaffected form. To that end, I instructed our videographers never to script a scene or to correct grammar or usage. We continued to follow that dictum in our editing and in our creating of transcripts and translations. All language is in its original form — exactly as a traveler will hear the language spoken.

As important as the authentic language is, its environment, the raw video footage, is even more important. When I was a novice teacher 15 years ago, I was already aware of the copyright difficulties that are inherent in trying to adapt footage to fit pedagogical purposes. For example, although I could easily videotape Italian TV segments off of the satellite, the "fair use" clause in copyright law allowed me to keep them, even for educational purposes, for only 30–45 days, meaning that my pedagogical material was being destroyed almost as soon as it was created. Purchased video cassettes of target-language films present their own difficulties as well. Although, as the purchaser, the institution can keep and use the video for years, one is not permitted to change the format, that is, edit little segments, take clips out of sequence, and so on. The holders of copyright frequently do understand what these constraints mean to educators; however, while some holders of copyright will privately allow their material to be used educationally, they are rarely willing to put that permission on paper. My solution to these roadblocks was to shoot my own video for my classroom use.

Here the question "why not just hire a professional?" is bound to arise. Indeed if one's goal is to obtain the clearest, best quality video possible, then hiring a professional videographer/film maker is the obvious choice. There are, however, tradeoffs involved when professionals enter into the equation. First of all, the professional's own perception of what should be captured and "exported" to us becomes an issue. This was a big issue in the late 80's when professional TV stations tried to provide material from their own archives and re-purpose the video for language learning. For example, one of RAI's (Italian public television) earliest attempts was a monthly videotape series that showcased some of what they deemed to be their most trendy feature stories of the month. Frequently the videos were filled with fashion shows, car races, soccer clips, or Italian-American events taking place in New York. The material was interesting, but practically useless for the language learner unless the word "runway" entered into one's everyday speech! It is natural to want to show the best of one's own country, but the professional videographer frequently does not understand the needs of a language learner any better than a commercial enterprise does. One of our international students, for example, has an uncle who is a professional filmmaker. He wanted to accompany his niece and help her with the video. He sent her back with a professional film that reflected all the scenes we asked to be included, but because he didn't think the people being videotaped were speaking correctly, he overlaid a soundtrack of music on the audio — making the project practically worthless. Because of cultural dynamics in that target country, the niece, whom we had trained and who understood what we needed, was not able to correct her uncle's misconceptions, and we had to re-shoot in that country the following summer.

Except for that particular incident, we have had success in training our international students to do videotaping in their home countries. The first FCFLRC publication, *The Five College Foreign Language Laserdisc Series* (originally from the University of Massachusetts Press and currently reconfigured for Web use on the LangMedia site) is, as its series title indicates, also video-based. The production of that series allowed us to perfect our video gathering technique. The challenge is this: to capture authentic scenes of interaction and instances of speech-making in a natural setting using non-professional informants. At the outset, this means eliminating professional videographers, intrusive microphones, light pods, and other contraptions that interfere with the basic speech-making. The only person who can penetrate the cultural environment of a target-language country without ruining the spontaneity of that environment is a native-speaking member of that target-language community. Thus instead of the more frequently used agenda of finding a videographer and training him or her in the culture of the country, we start with what we believe to be the most important component: a native-speaking member of the target culture and train that person to be a videographer. Our footage is not that of a professional soundstage, but it is authentic.

We have had much success training bright, international students from the Five Colleges to shoot the video. Because they are native-speakers of the target language and members of the target cultures, they fit right into the environment they are seeking to capture. They have friends and family members who are eager to help them with their project. By going to local enterprises, they are able to videotape the people with whom their families interact in everyday life. Using their and friends' families as liaisons, they are able to gain access to situations that would be forbidden to others. For example, a friend's father who is a bank president will arrange for the student to videotape someone doing business with a teller while a friend's physician mother will give a sample physical exam to the friend and discuss the various payment methods. A further advantage to employing international students as videographers is that the majority of these students have recently undergone the same types of learning processes in the US that we are trying to capture in the target country, so they have an innate sense of what is valuable material.

Because the FCFLRC is the home of the Five College Self-Instructional Language Program (the program that affords students the opportunity to study, in an independently directed format, languages that are not offered in the classroom on any of the five campuses), we are well acquainted with the international students in our community. In many cases, we have already taken care of the paperwork that allows them to work for us (checking visas and getting permissions signed by various deans of international students). Dozens of them are already employed by the FCFLRC as native-speaking conversation partners for the FCSILP. Being hired by the FCSILP is viewed as an honor in the international student community; for every position we offer, we may have as many as 10 applicants, so we are able to choose the best qualified students to work for the program. Through the training that they receive from us, and through their work with the Five College student population, these international students have a good understanding of what it is that foreigners need to know about their home countries

Training a bright, enthusiastic student to capture the needed video is much easier than it might appear. The first task is to identify a potentially good videographer. In the second half of every semester, we send out advertisements to our international students and their associations identifying the countries/cultures/languages for which we need student videographers. The student need not have had experience with either cameras or Web design but must be willing to learn. S/he should be planning on spending the major part of vacation in the home country because getting the videotape shot takes a lot longer than one might think. The student must also be free of political or ethnic prejudices, which is fairly easy to determine in a half-hour, in-person interview. During my first video project, one of the students brought in her video, and I immediately noticed that some of the best footage had no sound track. She explained that she turned off the camera microphone whenever she encountered individuals of a certain ethnicity because they "didn't matter" in her country. I have learned to include conversation topics in the interview stage that would reveal any such lurking prejudices on the part of the students that might impact the video shoot. After we have met all of our videographer candidates, we outline our shoots, trying to distribute equipment among a variety of countries and/or in diverse regions of a particular country. Therefore, if we have five students applying to go to India and four are from the south and one is from the north, we will choose one from the south and one from the north so as to get a variety of footage. Another consideration is whether or not the student will be able to work with us the following semester. A student with video experience who will be spending the following year on junior year abroad might not be selected if another reasonably qualified student will be returning to the area because we have found it desirable to have one student working with us from start to finish. Each student receives a stipend of $250 dollars for the video shoot and reimbursement for incidental expenses. We pay $10/hour for editing work in our office upon their return, and they usually work 5 or 6 hours per week for a semester or two, depending on how much footage they have shot and on what type of font their target language requires. Getting a site together in Thai takes longer than a similar site in Swahili. Once we have selected our student videographers, we start training them. We have learned that, to facilitate training, the learners should work with us and with student videographers who have experience from previous shoots.

We begin in the FCFLRC by teaching the student videographer the basics of video shooting and editing. I try to get students in groups of at least two so that they can use each other as guinea pigs, and I get one of our student videographers from a previous shoot to train them with me. These fellow students are frequently able to calm fears and answer questions about their experiences in their home countries. One of the most common concerns is the reaction of the target country's customs officials to the in-coming equipment; in reality, this rarely poses a problem, and the experienced students can quickly allay concerns. As for the quality of footage itself, we discuss it theoretically as a group, and I set up hypothetical scenarios to see if our trainees can spot a potential pitfall. Once it is clearly understood what makes video good or bad, usable or unusable (in terms of sound, light, surroundings, size of focus area, color), the students do some practice shooting in the office, and then we look at the video and discuss its merits or problems. Then we send the students out of the office with the camcorder, a tripod, and an external microphone with earphones (for sound control) to shoot signs (immovable objects), crowds of people, and small conversations. The experienced student videographer accompanies them. They return to our office after an hour or so, and again we all look at their footage together. The most frequent initial problems are camera angle, shadows and glares, unsightly, extrinsic material (such as foul graffiti written on a phone booth), and unflattering poses. At this time, we discuss the content of the captured conversations. Since we are potentially interested in putting the finished video on the Web, we don't want anyone giving out personal information, such as home address or phone number. Most students are savvy enough to have already understood such potential dangers. After this beginning session with us in our Center, the student returns to his/her home campus to make a short (2- to 5-minute) video on a chosen subject. We suggest that the student take advantage of the equipment to make a video for the family showing the dorm, meeting some roommates or friends, and so on. In this way, the student has a vested interest in making the video the best possible because it will be a gift for the family. Having captured the footage, the student then returns to view it in the Center and discuss positive and negative aspects of the footage. By the end of the training, the student videographer is well prepared (mechanically speaking, at least) to return home for either summer or winter vacation and capture the required footage. We send a sheet of video tips along with the student in case questions arise on site (Appendix A).

While the physical process of shooting usable video is important to the finished product, content is equally important. We approach content in several ways. First, the Center has developed a list of suggested topics and situations (Appendix B) that are, in general, pertinent to every culture (e.g., proper greetings and partings), with the emphasis on behavioral standards, body language, and appropriate usage of formulas or honorifics. In Swahili, for example, one must thoroughly understand the importance of including the "Shikamoo" (reply "Marahaba") in a greeting exchange between parties of differing ages. The word "Shikamoo" must appear somewhere in the greeting conversation, which can be long and complex or relatively brief and to the point. In Hindi, on the other hand, body language is as important to the greeting as the words themselves (the younger person bows lower than the elder, and younger males should make a praying motion with their hands while aiming their hands toward their feet as they bow). We discuss all of the topics with our students, trying to make them connoisseurs of their own culture. Because their own introduction to U.S. customs is so fresh in their memories, they usually understand immediately what we are looking for and, indeed, are quick to add their own suggestions to augment our list. We tell all students that our list of topics is only a suggestion list. If they deem any item on our list to be inappropriate for whatever reason, they should omit it. Similarly, they should feel free to add elements that are culturally specific and which we would not have known to include. During the first conversation we had with one of our young women from Bulgaria, she said that the most important thing to illustrate to foreigners in Bulgaria was the difference between nodding (which means "no" in Bulgaria) and shaking one's head (to indicate "yes"). Most students think of such unique cultural aspects even while in our Center in the US; by the time they arrive in their home countries, they've thought of all sorts of necessary shots.

Although the students arrive in their country with letters of introduction from me (as well as the all-important letter for customs regarding ownership of all the equipment), we have found that the video shoots run more smoothly if the students don't need to use those letters. We encourage them to do their shoots in the areas and establishments frequented by their families on an everyday basis. The key to success is being "inconspicuous." If they ask the local baker if they can film mom buying the family's daily bread as she does every day of her life, the baker will say "sure." If they ask someone in a large supermarket to be allowed to do the same thing, the manager is inevitably summoned, and permission is denied (no matter how many letters of introduction they have from me).

The students also have to pay attention to everyday, volatile, political occurrences in their countries. The student we sent to one country recently had a basically unsuccessful shoot because her visit just happened to coincide with a rash of terrorism and terrorist threats in that city. So each time she took out her camcorder, she was approached by police because, of course, all the prime points of interest for our video — banks, train station, post office — could also have been of interest to terrorist groups. So this student ended up having much more contact with police than she wanted, and she returned with practically no outside shots. Conversely, sometimes positive interest by locals can be just as destructive. A student found that, by the time she had set up her tripod, she had gathered such a crowd that she couldn't do the shoot. Her solution was to leave the tripod at home (creating difficulties in the editing stages) and simply whip the camera out from under her coat and shoot her video before interested bystanders could comprehend what was happening. Our students do understand that their safety and comfort level are the most important considerations to us; if something makes them uncomfortable for whatever reason, they should not do it. Fortunately, in most instances, the video shoot is a positive experience for the international students; they have a lot of fun, they bond with family and friends in creating the video, and they enjoy gaining a new sense of their countries.

The next step in our process happens when the students return to our Center with their video (an average of six hours of video). We make working copies of their video cassettes and then set them up with a monitor and film counter to log their materials. The log looks like this:

1:12:21	Grocery store – buying groceries
1:14:10	Grocery store – paying
1:14:30	Grocery store – paying and getting change (best)
1:14:58	Public transportation – getting in, paying
1:15:24	Public transportation – paying, asking driver

We have found that having the videographer make his/her own log saves time although, in a pinch, another native speaker can work on someone else's video. After the logging is complete, digital editing begins. Each video clip is designed as an individual, stand-alone segment complete with transcript in the original target language and transcript in English. Creating the transcripts elicits the type of dilemmas one can easily imagine. Do we try to translate "cannoli" or describe it or leave it alone? What should we do with grammatically incorrect speech? How should we handle those regional dialects? Our solution is to write a target-language transcript that represents exactly what is being said on the video (grammatically correct or not) and to add parenthetical explanations (in both versions of the transcript) that explain the meaning of slang, dialect, or those words that are not easily translated. In the end, we try to remain true to our goal of illustrating language as it *is* spoken and not as it *should be* spoken.

Once we have edited the clips and written the transcripts, we are ready to import that material onto the appropriate Web page. We record basic audio phrases for the audio part of the page (using SoundForge in our office), and we scan images of tickets, phone cards, menus, and so on for the section of stills. The last item that goes on a Web page is the paragraph explaining the basics of the topic under discussion. We write the paragraphs with the help of the international students. For example, the paragraph from "How to Use a Pay Phone" in Hungary reads

> Pick up the receiver and then insert either your coin or your pre-purchased phone card. Note that phones will be designed to take either a coin or a card and not both. If you insert coins, you will not get change at the end of your call, so pay attention to how much you are inserting. If you use a phone card, it will remain in the phone card slot until you have finished your conversation. After you hang up, remember to take your phone card with you. Basic instructions about phone usage, costs, and emergency numbers are posted inside the phone booths.

Eventually we have a consulting professor of the target language and culture look over the entire site for errors, but only after we have had several international students proof the target-language text. Finally, we add the language site to the LangMedia homepage and launch it.

Fortunately, these group productions are great fun for all involved, especially for the international students who not only bond with family and friends whom they had missed during their year in the States but who also learn a lot about their own countries. At the end of their work with us, these students completed evaluation forms, some of which are quoted below. Because of issues of student confidentiality, I cannot identify our students either by name or by country, but their observations are worth noting.

Many of the students found that walking around with a camcorder automatically made them a famous director in the minds of on-lookers: "... people thought that I was from MTV or 'Candid Camera.' They were convinced that I was some famous or budding film director... I couldn't convince them otherwise and some followed me from shoot to shoot for hours!" Some students expected a negative reaction from people asked to be in the videos and were pleasantly surprised. "I didn't know what exactly to expect... at most, I expected people to be camera shy. But what I got was completely the opposite. As soon as I would step out onto the street with my equipment, I would attract stares. By the time I took out my camera and decided what it was I wanted to film, there was a crowd of 20 or 30 people around me trying to get into the picture. People were more than happy to oblige me... and the spectators felt free to shout out comments and suggestions to the 'actors.'" Other students who expected cooperation were disappointed with people's reactions. "While shooting this video, I realized how 'particular' we are... I noticed that we are not used to seeing cameras around and that we are suspicious and don't want to appear in someone else's video…" Most students were encouraged by the attitudes they encountered, and even those who seemed suspicious at first, gave in after being asked nicely. "[Some] people would act tough with me in the beginning, but if I made it seem like they were doing me a favor and if I asked them humbly enough, they would melt… and would usually invite me to sit with them and drink tea."

Probably the more important insights gained by the students were about their own country and the image it presents to foreigners. One student noted, "After doing this project, I noticed that in my country we have different customs (from the US) — how we act in a restaurant, how we board a bus — and that those little details are what make us who we are." Another student remembered how difficult her first few weeks in the US were and tried to put herself in the position of someone new to her country. "When I first came here, it was more the small things that I noticed. For example, I didn't know how to put a dollar bill into a coke machine, and the first time I tried, it spat it back out at me (I must have put it in upside down). I was so embarrassed because there was someone waiting behind me! My everyday experience at college in the US made me more sensitive to what people might find different or strange, or just simply might not know how to do in my country. Being asked 'cash or charge' by an irate salesperson can be scary when you are paying for the first time… I tried to include details of how to do basic things in my video."

Certainly LangMedia as it is currently conceived, and in fact, most of the video work that we have done in the FCFLRC during the past 10 years, would not be possible without the active participation of our fleets of international students. Not only have the students bonded with their video helpers, but so too have we in the Center. We have gotten to know the families and friends of our students through their videos. When parents arrive for graduation, they seem like old friends. Those involved in making the videos in the target countries are eager to see the Web site, and they feel that they have a vested interest in making it the best it can be. We have had target-country individuals contact us to tell us that a particular type of phone card is not longer available so we can adjust the site or that there is a new type of express train that needs to be included. We feel that we have little enclaves of friends all over the world thanks to this project. Still, the people who gain the most through the video shooting are the international students themselves. "I would definitely recommend this [experience] to a friend. You get to meet all sorts of people while doing the job… and it slows you down so that you can get a real look at your country. Sometimes we take things for granted and do a lot of complaining. But there is a lot of beauty at home, even in the things that we crib about."

APPENDIX A:
REMINDERS AND QUICK TIPS FOR YOUR VIDEO SHOOT

1. Take time to set up the shoot — look at the viewfinder to check for problems. Put on the headphones to listen for problems.
2. Change things if there are problems. Example: if you can't see someone because of light problems maybe moving him/her will help.
3. Use the tripod.
4. Use the microphone.
5. Don't move the camera while you are shooting, leave it in one place.
6. Check the lighting situation — make sure people are not in front of or next to large bright things (walls or especially windows). You will not be able to see their faces if they are.
7. Let the camera run for 5 seconds before and after the situation you are taping begins and ends.
8. Turn off any special features on the camera (no time or date display).
9. Remember: we are focusing on the language. Language situations and signs are very important.
10. Have fun!

APPENDIX B:
FIVE COLLEGE FOREIGN LANGUAGE VIDEO ARCHIVE —
CHECKLIST FOR VIDEOGRAPHERS

Note: Not all of these items may apply in every country, and in some countries there may be filming restrictions or demands of etiquette which limit the kind of footage you may take on a topic. You will need to adjust accordingly. Also be on the lookout for topics/situations unique to your country which a visitor would find very helpful or necessary to know.

Telephones
— still shots of public phones and signs related to public phones (sellers of phone cards, etc.)
— videotape a demonstration of how to use a public phone
    — show for example how to insert the phone card
    — close-ups of instructions on the phone or the phone booth
    — have someone make a short phone call to a friend
— at least 3 videos of friends or family members making standard types of phone calls, such as
    — calling a home or office and asking to speak with a specific person
    — calling a hotel to make reservations
    — calling an operator/directory assistance
    — making a long distance and/or collect call
    — calling a friend and having an informal conversation
    — calling someone and having a formal conversation (for example, with a friend's parent)

Banks and/or money exchanges
— signs for banks, money exchanges, ATMs
— if possible bring back a copy of form that you have to fill out to exchange money
— if possible video tape someone exchanging money or getting money from an ATM machine

Post offices
— stills of signs for post offices and for various services, windows, and instructions inside the post office
    — what services can you get at the post office (stamps, packages, phone, etc.)?
— postal boxes around the city: what do they look like? get still shots.
— bring back examples of common stamps
— video tape someone doing business at the post office (mailing a letter or package, buying stamps, etc.)

Signs for public services
- police station
- hospitals and clinics
    - where would you go for a serious emergency?
    - where would you go for a less serious health matter?
- fire stations
- trash and recycling containers (where do you throw things away?)

Toilets
- signs for male and female facilities
- costs and/or tipping customs for using public facilities, if there is an attendant videotape the interaction with the attendant
- show how the toilets work (such as how do they flush?) and other proper etiquette for washing hands, etc.

Local transportation: Bus, subway, taxi, trains, rickshaws, any other local forms of transportation
- what do each of the major forms of public transportation look like? get still shots
- signs for public transportation such as bus stops, subway stops, train, etc.
- bring back examples of tickets and schedules
- video of how/where to buy tickets/tokens, how to get on and off, validate a ticket, etc.
    - show someone buying a ticket, paying the driver, and/or negotiating prices for the various forms of transport
- videotape someone getting a taxi (either on the street, taxi stop, or calling on the phone)
- signs pedestrians would need to know (walk, don't walk, etc.)

Train stations
- signs for the train station
- signs inside the train station (tracks, arrival and departure information., ticket counters, etc.)
- boards/announcements of track assignments and arrival and departure times
- visitors information center/traveler's aid, etc.
- videotape someone either buying a ticket or asking for information about schedules and prices

Airports
- signs indicating "airport"
- signs inside an airport (ticketing, baggage claim, gates, toilets, etc.)
- if possible, customs forms in the local language
- anything else you can comfortably videotape that shows travelers what to expect at the airport

Cars
— signs for car rental places
— videotape someone renting a car and/or asking for information about car rentals
— essential traffic signs: stoplights, stop signs, speed limits, etc.
— signs for parking locations
— gas station signs, show someone getting gas at a station

Hotels
— find a cooperative hotel desk clerk and video tape someone making reservations or checking into the hotel
    — have the person ask about rooms of different types, such as
        — one person, two persons
        — private bath, bath down the hall
        — asking about cost
        — asking about whether or not breakfast is included

Restaurants
— videotape the process of eating in different types of restaurants/food establishments
    — choose the cheaper and medium priced places students would tend to eat
    — for restaurants show seating, ordering, getting the bill, paying, etc.
    — include street vendors, little shops that serve prepared foods, fast food places, etc.
— get still shots of signs for various types of eating places
— menus (bring back if possible)

Shopping
— make videos of people shopping in various types of food shops, markets, supermarkets
    — places where you would buy common foods, such as
        — bread
        — fruits and vegetables
        — milk products
        — meat
— get video of someone buying fruit: who picks it up and bags it, the customer or the vendor? would the vendor be offended if the customer touched the fruit?
— make a video of someone shopping in a pharmacy, show something such as
    — buying aspirin/pain relievers
    — buying medication with a prescription
— show someone buying something in a different kind of market or store
    — if it is the custom to bargain for prices show someone bargaining for something

Common verbal exchanges: Make short videos showing these types of situations
- asking someone for directions
- greetings and good-byes (formal and informal, appropriate honorifics, motions or gestures)
    - also include proper introductions and responses when meeting new people
    - proper manners when visiting in a private home, how do you greet the hosts if you are the guest, etc.
    - proper manners between younger people and older people (children and adults, or adults with older adults)
- proper manners at the table (for instance example, passing food at the table, pleases and thank yous, etc.)
- asking someone "what time it is?" or discussing with someone what time something is scheduled

Cultural specific etiquette
- customs appropriate for your culture, such as
    - are there places you have to take off your shoes before entering?
    - proper forms of dress for certain settings
    - who's allowed where (men, women, children)
- tipping: who should be tipped?

Laundry
- How would someone who is visiting do their laundry (or have someone else do it)?

Computer cafes: If these exist or any other way of public access to the Internet
- if Internet clubs or cafes exist, videotape someone asking about prices and/or "buying time" to use the computers

Entertainment
- What are common forms of entertainment, especially for students. You could for example show someone buying movie tickets, going to a club or coffee place, etc.

Note: There are things that we simply can't know to suggest. Try to think about your country through the eyes of someone who has never been there before (e.g., a friend from your school who came to visit). What practical things about being in your country would they need to learn in order to manage well and to behave in appropriate ways? We will be able to explain some of these things on the Web site, but it is really helpful if you can get demonstrations on video. Also, there may be aspects of life in your country that you have special access to because of family members or friend's employment. For example, one student whose mother is a physician was able to videotape her sister going to her mother as a "patient" looking for treatment for her sore throat. Another person had an uncle who owned a restaurant and he let them do an extended "inside the restaurant" scene. Make use of those connections if you have them.

Norman J. Peterson
Montana State University-Bozeman

A NEW PARADIGM FOR LESS COMMONLY TAUGHT LANGUAGES: THE ARABIC LANGUAGE AND MIDDLE EAST/NORTH AFRICAN CULTURAL STUDIES PROGRAM

Providing instruction in less-commonly-taught languages is an enormous challenge to most U.S. colleges and universities. Although many institutions recognize the growing importance of languages such as Arabic, Japanese, Korean, Mandarin, Russian, and Swahili, the costs of adding these languages to the curriculum through traditional instructional approaches built around permanent faculty positions are overwhelming. As a result, students attending most U.S. institutions are limited to a small set of traditional European languages in choosing a language to study. There is no reason to believe that this situation will improve, at least in the short-term. In fact, it is more likely that faculty positions in foreign languages will decrease rather than increase. The reality is that unless new approaches are developed, these less-commonly-taught languages will never be available to students at most institutions.

Because of this, the choices facing students intent on learning a less-commonly-taught language are far from optimal. They can choose among a relatively few U.S. universities offering the language of their interest. They can attempt to put together some type of self-instructional program. Or they can elect to study abroad in a country in which the language is spoken, hopefully finding a program in which they can continue their studies in English while beginning an intensive language program.

If students attending institutions "across the fabric" of U.S. higher education are going to have access to important world languages, entirely new approaches need to be developed which can offer effective language instruction on a more affordable basis. This is the goal of the Arabic Language and Middle East/North African Cultural Studies Program (hereafter referenced as the "Arabic Project"). The project has been developed by Montana State University-Bozeman, working closely with the University of Washington in Seattle, Al Akhawayn University in Morocco, and a consortium of participating institutions. Critical funding support to develop the program has been provided by the National Security Education Program.

Peterson, N. (2002). A new paradigm for less commonly taught languages: The Arabic Language and Middle East/North African Cultural Studies Program. In C. A. Spreen (Ed.), *New technologies and language learning: Cases in the less commonly taught languages* (Technical Report #25; pp. 135–144). Honolulu, HI: University of Hawai'i, Second Language Teaching & Curriculum Center.

CONFIGURING AVAILABLE LANGUAGE RESOURCES

The starting point for the project is this: If it is not realistic for our institutions (or most others) to afford the basic resource needed to offer Arabic or other less-commonly-taught languages (namely, a permanent faculty position), what alternative resources are available which can be put together to provide an alternative instructional approach? In other words, are there other, more affordable resources for language education that can be configured into an effective program so that less-commonly-taught languages can become more-frequently-taught?

The institutions involved in the Arabic Project believe that the answer to this question is "yes" and that a solution lies in combining four alternative and readily available resources to create a new approach to university language instruction. These four resources are a) distance education technologies, b) faculty expertise located in regional foreign language centers, c) international students who are native speakers of the language, and d) study abroad opportunities in the countries in which the language is spoken. Many U.S. universities now have quality distance education facilities, including both synchronous interactive video classrooms and asynchronous computer access to the Internet and the World Wide Web. While most campuses lack faculty expertise in less-commonly-taught languages, there are a few universities throughout the US with national resource centers that have this expertise. Over half a million international students enroll in U.S. universities, many of whom are native speakers of these languages. Finally, many institutions have or can develop study abroad or exchange programs with institutions in the nations in which these languages are spoken. The Arabic Project combines these four ingredients into a new approach to offer Arabic language and cultural studies that over the last three years has proven to be highly successful.

In addition to the use of these alternative resources to provide the basis for teaching Arabic, the project design is based on three principals. An underlying assumption of the Arabic Project is that exclusive reliance on one alternative resource (such as a course taught completely online or only through foreign student TAs or only through study abroad) will not be highly successful. That is to say, none of the alternative resources identified is able to effectively stand on its own. The design of the Arabic Project is based on providing several mutually supportive instructional approaches. Another characteristic of the Arabic Project is integration of technology (including both synchronous and asynchronous elements) with more traditional elements (such as study abroad or use of TA's) to create a strong and effective program. Unfortunately, all too often those who administer traditional international programs shun new technologies as antithetical to the direct human interactions involved in exchange programs, while those enraptured with technology as frequently shun traditional program elements as old fashioned. A third feature of the program is the "seamless" integration between the language curriculum students follow on the home campus and the language program studied while abroad. Presently, in most cases there is little or no integration between the language programs students pursue on their home campuses and at their study sites abroad.

OVERVIEW OF THE PROGRAM

Through a design based on these principals that carefully integrates the four resources cited above, the Arabic Project offers the opportunity for students at participating institutions to take three or more years of Arabic language and culture.

Table 1. Outline of Arabic academic program by year

year 1	year 2	year 3–4
Students enroll in Modern Standard Arabic course on their home campus (4–5 credits/semester)	Students on exchange at Al Akhawayn University in Morocco	TAs on site offer 1 credit/semester conversation classes
Interactive video class with Univ. of Washington instructor 2 hours/week	"Seamless" continuation of Modern Standard Arabic	New online courses being developed by Al Akhawayn University
Instruction by native speaker TA on site 2–3 hours/week	Additional courses taught in English to continue progress toward degree requirements at home institution	

During year 1, students enroll in Introduction to Modern Standard Arabic, a course delivered through to their home campuses via a combination of interactive video classes originating at the University of Washington in Seattle and TA instruction from a native Arabic speaking student in residence. In year 2 students who remain in the program study at Al Akhawayn University in Morocco where they continue their study of Modern Standard Arabic while they take other courses toward their degrees taught in English. In years 3 and 4, the students can participate in conversation courses led by the TA's and will soon be able to take upper division online Arabic courses taught by Al Akhawayn faculty.

This instructional program is built around a consortium of universities developed specifically for the Arabic Project with a unique division of responsibilities (see Figure 1).

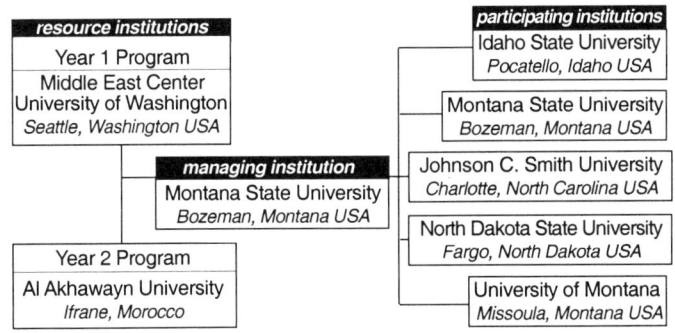

Figure 1. Arabic Project institutional organization chart

Two institutions (the University of Washington in Seattle and Al Akhawyn University in Morocco (are "resource institutions," providing the academic expertise for the program. Montana State University-Bozeman serves as the "managing institution," coordinating all activity. A set of "participating institutions" (listed above) offer the academic program provided by the resource institutions to their students.

With this overview of the program in mind, it may be useful to return to the four alternative resources that underlie it, looking at each one in somewhat greater detail.

USING EDUCATIONAL TECHNOLOGIES

Distance education technologies are a critical component of the Arabic Project. Interactive video classrooms, coupled with Internet connections and Web resources, make it possible to link language learners on the campuses of participating institutions with faculty expertise at our U.S. resource institution at the University of Washington. The Arabic Project uses these technologies to create a single virtual classroom with the instructor at the University of Washington in Seattle and students at the participating institutions stretching from Idaho to North Carolina. Each semester the instructor holds two one-hour classes per week, simultaneously teaching students at all five locations. The classes are held in special interactive video classrooms, and all students can see, hear, and interact with the instructor. Figure 2 shows how this network is structured.

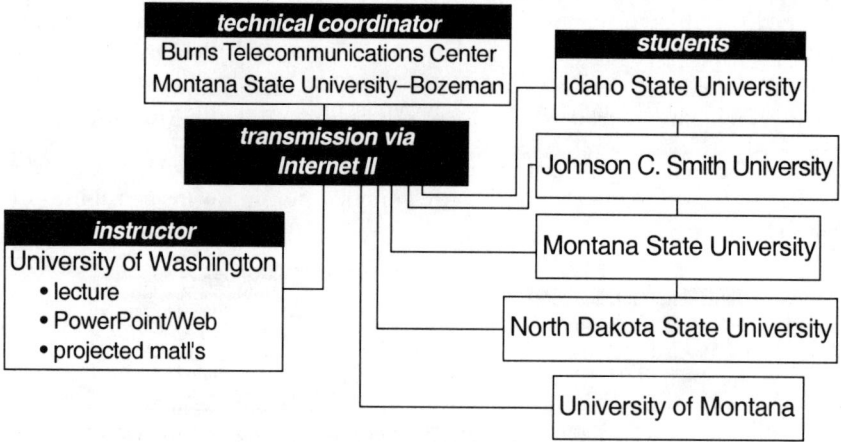

Figure 2. Arabic Project interactive video connections

The Arabic Project's virtual classroom spans three time zones. At the beginning of each academic year, it can include as many as 70 students although the usual number is closer to 50. While the virtual classroom is the foundation for the instructional program, the size of the class limits the amount of time and attention the instructor can give individual students. Similarly, the number of different locations linked limits the ability of the instructor to interact with students. It is our experience that five locations is probably the maximum number of sites that can work with a single instructor at one time. While the overall audio and video quality is quite good, the demands of Arabic language education are very high, particularly regarding audio quality, and these demands push the limits of interactive video. All of these factors combine to make the TAs' role at each participating institution particularly important to the success of the program.

During the first 3 years of the project, the virtual classroom has been linked together by means of telephonic connections using a commercial "bridging" company. While certainly workable, this approach is fairly expensive, costing about $32,000 per year, and the overall quality is only marginally good enough to carry the course content. To overcome these cost and quality issues, the project has been seeking a better solution and starting fall semester 2001 the interactive video classroom sessions have been transmitted through broad band Internet connections rather than through traditional compressed video telephone line transmissions. With the advent of broadband Internet capabilities such as Internet II, it has become possible to route interactive video sessions through the Internet using devices known as "polycomm boxes," achieving tremendous cost savings while increasing audio and video quality. While this may seem to be a small technical issue, it is critical to both the quality of the instructional program and achieving the project's goal of an affordable approach to language instruction.

In addition to the virtual classroom, the Arabic Project also makes extensive use of the Internet and its Arabic studies Web site (www.arabicstudies.edu), fulfilling vital communication roles in keeping the instructor, the TAs, and the students linked together. The project's Web site also provides an important learning resource for the students, including information on Middle Eastern and North African culture and links to other information, as well as information on the project to others interested in the instructional model.

NATIVE SPEAKER INTERNATIONAL STUDENTS

As emphasized above, the native Arabic speaking TAs in residence at each participating institution are a critical component of the program. While the virtual classroom is cool and high-tech, because of the limitations discussed above (audio/video quality and constraints in dealing with a large number of students at several different locations), students come to rely heavily on the TAs. In fact, in student evaluations, the TAs are consistently ranked as the most important part of the program.

For decades, international educators in the United States have felt that foreign students on our campuses, which now exceed half a million, are an underutilized resource. The Arabic Project has identified an important role they can play in language education during their period of study in the US. In the case of Arabic, there are a lot of possible TAs on our campuses. According to the latest data published by the Institute of International Education, there are almost 34,000 students from the countries of the Middle East now studying in the United States, and there are many additional Arabic speakers on our campuses from North Africa and other nations.

The participating institutions in the Arabic Project offer a small honorarium to the TAs on their campus to compensate them for their services. While the amount is modest, it is a welcome piece of income for these students and is more desirable than typical on-campus jobs to which foreign students are limited under the terms of their student visas.

While these students can play a great role in enhancing U.S. skills in Arabic and other less-commonly-taught languages, they must be trained carefully and they must work under the supervision of faculty who are experts in language teaching. As is well known in the foreign language teaching world, being a native speaker of a language does not mean at all that one is able to teach it. For this reason, the Arabic Project has put particular attention on training the TAs. Each year prior to the start of the fall semester, all the TAs are brought together with faculty from the University of Washington for a week-long TA training program.

Although the TAs principal responsibilities focus on teaching the students in the first-year class, they also play an important role in helping students returning from the second-year program in Morocco. Arabic Project students returning from Morocco are typically highly motivated to maintain and improve their Arabic. This is a major challenge for the project, but having the TAs teach a special one credit hour conversation class for the Morocco returnees has proven to be a useful solution to this problem. To offer additional options to students returning from the second year program, Al Akhawayn University faculty are now working on developing several Internet-based courses which students will be able to take in the future, enabling students to continue their Arabic at more advanced levels working online with the faculty they know from their time in Morocco.

FACULTY BASED IN TITLE VI AND OTHER REGIONAL CENTERS

The third main resource around which the Arabic Project is built is faculty expertise located in centers devoted to foreign language and area studies around the United States. The Arabic Project has been extremely fortunate to have the enthusiastic commitment of the faculty of the Near Eastern Languages and Civilization Department and the Middle East Center at the University of Washington. The project would not have been possible without them. Ultimately it is their expertise in the Arabic language and how to teach it, as well as their knowledge of the cultures of the Arab world, that is the fundamental knowledge base of the program. For the Arabic Project, there are two University of Washington faculty members who play fundamental roles. First, there is an instructor, who teaches the virtual classroom, works with the students and TAs on a daily basis, and administers tests, assigns grades, and so forth. For the last two years Mr. Ahmed Souaiaia has ably filled this position. Second, Associate Professor Terri Deyoung serves as a senior faculty supervisor. Professor Deyoung has been involved in the project from its launch and she has made extraordinary contributions in developing the curriculum, and instructional strategies, and in supervising the instructor.

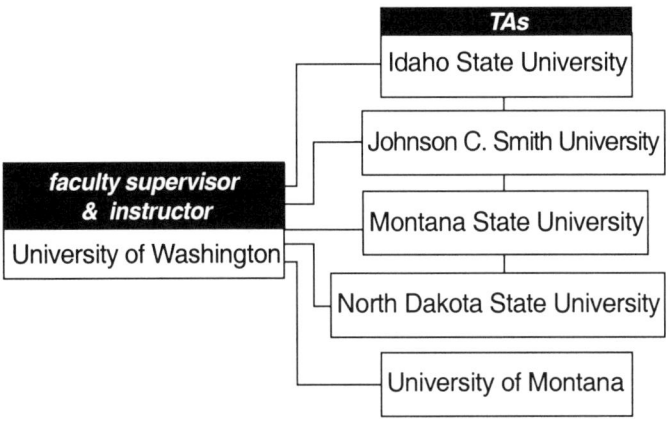

Figure 3. Structure of year 1 academic program

These key faculty resources fit into the overall instructional structure for the year 1 portion of the project as illustrated in Figure 3.

In addition, on most campuses a member of the foreign language faculty also supervises and provides support for the TA.

Many of the foreign language centers around the United States that have faculty with this kind of expertise are recipients of Department of Education Title VI support. The Arabic Project model offers a particular advantage to such centers because they have obligations to conduct outreach activities within their regions as a condition of their federal funding. The Arabic Project's design offers Title VI centers particularly attractive and effective outreach opportunities.

STUDY ABROAD

The fourth of the basic resources around which the Arabic Project is built is study abroad. Of course, there is nothing new in language students going abroad to further their language studies. What is different about study abroad in the Arabic Project is that it is tightly integrated into the design of the program. For most language students, there is little or no articulation between their language studies on the home campus and abroad. In general, students select a study abroad program that is entirely independent of the language program on campus. Even when the study abroad program is sponsored by the student's home institution, it is typically not the case that the language program offered abroad is coordinated closely with the program on the home campus. In the language-learning model developed by the Arabic Project, the study abroad component is tightly integrated into the overall program. To the greatest extent possible, the project attempts to create a "seamless" transition between the year 1 home campus course and the year 2 Morocco experience. The same text is used for both years and students will begin in Morocco on the page they left off at their home university.

The choice of the study site is particularly important for a program such as the Arabic Project. Al Akhawayn's characteristics make it an ideal location for Arabic Project students. The University is an English language institution, enabling Arabic Project students to take courses toward their majors while continuing their Arabic studies. Since the students in the program are not Arabic majors, this is an extremely important feature. Certainly few students would elect the study abroad option if they could not continue to make study progress toward their degrees while pursuing further studies in Arabic. In addition, health and safety issues must be taken very seriously in planning the study abroad program for students wanting to pursue Arabic. Morocco is an ideal location for the students in this regard, offering one of the most stable and safe environments in the Arab world.

Actually, the study abroad program is organized as a student exchange between Al Akhawayn University and the participating institutions in order to make study abroad more accessible for students from both the US and Morocco. Since Al Akhawayn is a private university with fairly high tuition, an exchange makes the study abroad program more affordable for U.S. students in the program. On the other hand, by including room and board benefits in the exchange, the program makes study in the US more affordable for Moroccan students, since high living costs in the US, coupled with the current strong U.S. dollar, are a major barrier to studying on a U.S. campus.

Montana State, acting as the project's managing partner, administers an exchange clearinghouse for this purpose, conducting selection, orientation, and other services for outgoing students and placing Al Akhawayn students at the participating institutions based on students' preferences together with the need to maintain exchange balances.

Future plans call for Al Akhawayn University to initiate a Certificate Program for students involved in the Arabic Project, providing formal recognition of the Arabic skills of students completing the year 2 program. This is a useful role for Al Akhawayn University in the project's consortial structure, obviating the need for the individual participating institutions to establish separate minors or certificate programs.

INITIAL OUTCOMES

Over the last three academic years, the Arabic Project has been offering students the opportunity to study Modern Standard Arabic and to learn about the cultures of the Middle East and North Africa using this innovative new approach. Results are very encouraging. Although energetic recruiting and outreach is needed with students to reach enrollment targets, participating institutions have been able to find the critical mass of students (between 5 and 20) interested in taking the first year course. Attrition rates during the first year have been within the range expected for Arabic programs taught through traditional methods. Students in year 1 do as well or better on mid-term and final examinations as their counterparts taking Arabic in a traditional classroom. Those completing year 1 have done well on the ACTFL Arabic proficiency examination, normally scoring from Novice High to Intermediate Mid. A substantial proportion of students completing year 1 elect to continue into the year 2 program in Morocco. Those returning from Morocco are highly motivated to continue to develop their Arabic and to find other opportunities to pursue their interests in the Arab World. Thus, those involved in the Arabic Project are increasingly confident in the instructional model. Everything we know so far leads us to believe that the model provides a highly effective method to teach Arabic and, we believe, other languages that are not typically taught on U.S. campuses as well.

MOVING TOWARD SELF-SUFFICIENCY

The next critical step for the Arabic Project concerns the financial side of the program. Since its inception, the program has been able to rely on substantial funding from the National Security Education Program's institutional grant program. This funding has been critical to the development of the program. However, the Arabic Project will only be able to prove its importance as an alternative model for offering less-commonly-taught languages if and when it is able to operate without such external resources. The underlying concept of the program is that the resources upon which the project is based are affordable and can together form a self-sustaining program. Making this a reality is perhaps the Arabic Project's greatest challenge.

It is a challenge that is attainable, and here is how. As the project moves toward self-sufficiency, it is requiring participating campuses to begin to assume responsibility for the program's costs, drawing upon the tuition paid by students enrolled in the Arabic program. The first step toward this goal has already been completed. All participating campuses are paying the salaries for their TA from local resources. Participating campuses are also already paying the local costs associated with the interactive video classes.

There are four other costs that must be transferred from NSEP support over the coming two years. The most significant of these is the costs associated with the virtual interactive video classroom. As mentioned in the technology discussion above, the effort here is not primarily to transfer these costs to the participating institutions, but to dramatically decrease the costs by changing the technology. As mentioned above, starting in the fall semester 2001, the interactive video classroom sessions have been transmitted through Internet II rather than through costly telephone lines. Although the mid- to long-term cost structure of Internet II use remains to be worked out, this change will reduce transmission costs dramatically. Although specialized electronic equipment (generally referred to as "polycomm" boxes) is needed, there are no costs currently assessed for transmitting the interactive audio/video through Internet II. The other costs which need to be brought into a self-sufficient funding scheme are the costs for the instructor and faculty supervisor at the University of Washington, the administrative costs incurred by Montana State as the managing partner, and some smaller scale costs for items such as the TA training program and small travel scholarships currently offered to students to help meet costs for the year 2 program in Morocco. Plans call for these costs to be absorbed in several ways, including tapping tuition dollars from participating institutions, using support available from Title VI funds for outreach activities, and some modest fundraising efforts from companies interested in promoting positive business relations with the Middle East.

CONCLUSION

The Arabic Project represents an exciting new way to make less commonly taught languages available to students across the fabric of U.S. higher education, not just to students who happen to be attending a relatively small number of elite, specialized institutions. By combining several resources which either are already available on our campuses (such as international students who are native speakers of the languages and quality interactive video classrooms) or those which are easily attainable (such as exchange partnerships with institutions in the nations in which these languages are spoken), the Arabic Project hopes to point the way to a new paradigm for language instruction. This new paradigm hopes to offer a way that languages such as Arabic can be offered in an effective but affordable program by institutions across the country, institutions that realistically will never have the resources for permanent faculty positions focused on Arabic or other critical world languages not typically taught on U.S. campuses.

ABOUT THE CONTRIBUTORS

SCOTT BRILL has been research engineer with the University of Arizona's Computer Aided Language Instruction Group and Critical Languages Program for 12 years. He is the lead software developer of *MaxAuthor* and is project coordinator for the *Critical Languages Series* CD-ROMs. He received his BSEE from Carnegie-Mellon University. His current research interest is CALL for less commonly taught languages, especially on the Internet.

YUN DU is a software developer at Venngo, a Toronto-based software engineering firm that creates e-business applications. Her dissertation for the Ph.D. in Information and Communication Sciences at the University of Hawai'i treats the development and delivery of Web-based language learning environments.

ALEXANDER DUNKEL is NASILP's executive director, and is the founding director of the Critical Languages Program at the University of Arizona. He has participated in three NSEP grants, including the current "Expanding the National Capacity to Author and Produce Courseware in the Less Commonly Taught Languages," for which he is principal investigator. Professor Dunkel has taught Russian language, literature, and culture courses for the past thirty-nine years, interpreted for the U.S. State Department, and participated in US–Soviet/Russian Federation exchanges.

STEPHEN FLEMING is instructor in Technology for Foreign Language Education in the College of Languages, Linguistics and Literature at the University of Hawai'i at Mānoa. He has taught at UH for the past 13 years, and prior to that was a translator and editor for the Chinese Literature Press in Beijing. For the past 5 years, under grants from the National Security Education Program, he has developed models for distance education in less commonly taught languages using interactive television and Web technologies, and has also authored self-instructional software for intermediate-to-advanced Mandarin Chinese.

RHODALYNE GALLO-CRAIL is a language instructor at Northern Illinois University in DeKalb, Illinois, where she teaches beginning and intermediate Tagalog. She also helps develops the language activities for the Tagalog Web site. Her previous teaching experience includes 10 years of teaching ESL at the elementary and adult levels and doing teacher training and development. Her research interests are in the areas of language acquisition, sociolinguistics, and classroom pedagogy. She received her MA in Linguistics from Ohio University, Athens.

DAVID HIPLE is director of the Second Language Teaching and Curriculum Center and the Language Telecommunications Center at the University of Hawai'i at Mānoa; he has directed several distance education and distributed learning projects at UH. He has lived in Latin America and Eastern Europe and is a regular teacher trainer for Peace Corps internationally.

BRYAN KOHL is a multimedia production specialist with an academic background in cultural anthropology and sociolinguistics. Since 1998, he has directed production and post-production activities for multimedia projects at the University of Arizona's Critical Languages Program, including the Critical Languages Series. Bryan also has coordinated content reviews and beta and assessment testing of the Critical Languages Series.

ELIZABETH H. D. MAZZOCCO is Five College associate professor of Italian and director of the Five College Foreign Language Resource Center for Five Colleges, Inc (Amherst, Hampshire, Mount Holyoke, and Smith Colleges and the University of Massachusetts, Amherst). In addition to NSEP and others, she has received grants from FIPSE and the Andrew W. Mellon Foundation for her work in multimedia language pedagogy. She received her Ph.D. from Bryn Mawr College and is currently editor of the NASILP Journal. She has published the Five College Foreign Language Laserdisc Series and articles on the use of multimedia in language instruction and on Renaissance Italian literature.

NORMAN J. PETERSON is associate provost for International Education at Montana State University-Bozeman. In this capacity, he coordinates international programs at Montana State, including study abroad, curriculum development, foreign student services, university partnerships, and technical cooperation. He has professional interests in integrating new technologies and traditional international programs, and in increasing the coordination of study abroad in language education. He holds a Ph.D. in philosophy from the University of Colorado, Boulder, and has academic interests in post-Kantian European philosophy and aesthetic issues concerning film and photographic arts. Prior to assuming his position at Montana State, he held international positions at Georgetown University, the University of Maryland, and the University of Lancaster in the UK. He was the founding Executive Director of the Alliance for International Educational and Cultural Exchange in Washington DC and remains actively involved in national policy development relating to international education.

KEN PETERSEN holds a BA in English Language Instruction from Thiel College as well as an MA in Central Asian Languages and Literature from the University of Washington, Seattle. He is currently the internet administrator for the American Councils for International Education where he oversees the technical production of Web-based language learning applications for Russian and Central Asian Languages.

CAROL ANNE SPREEN is an assistant professor of International Education Policy in the Department of Education Policy and Leadership at the University of Maryland, College Park. She currently co-directs the International Center for Education Policy and Leadership and Human Values. Dr. Spreen received her Ph.D. from Columbia University in Comparative and International Education. Her research interests include international approaches to teaching and organizing curriculum, educational change, and policy reform. Prior to joining the University of Maryland faculty, Dr. Spreen was the assistant director of Institutional Grants at the National Security Education Program (NSEP). She was responsible for overall administration and monitoring of the NSEP grants program, and for organizing, collecting, and conducting research on the grant-funded initiatives. In this capacity, Dr. Spreen worked closely with university partners in conceptualizing, implementing, and evaluating international education initiatives at colleges and universities throughout the US.

ROBERT ZERWEKH is an associate professor of computer science at Northern Illinois University in DeKalb, Illinois where he regularly teaches courses in Java programming, database, and Enterprise server programming. He is one of the directors of the SEAsite project. Dr. Zerwekh's research interests are in the areas of Intelligent Tutoring Systems and Internet programming. He received a Ph.D. in Philosophy from the University of Illinois at Urbana and an MS in Computer Science from Northern Illinois University.

SLTCC
TECHNICAL REPORTS

The Technical Reports of the Second Language Teaching and Curriculum Center at the University of Hawai'i (SLTCC) report on ongoing curriculum projects, provide the results of research related to second language learning and teaching, and also include extensive related bibliographies. SLTCC Technical Reports are available through University of Hawai'i Press.

NEW TECHNOLOGIES AND LANGUAGE LEARNING: CASES IN THE LESS COMMONLY TAUGHT LANGUAGES

CAROL ANNE SPREEN (Editor)

In recent years, the National Security Education Program (NSEP) has supported an increasing number of programs for teaching languages using different technological media. This compilation of case study initiatives funded through the NSEP Institutional Grants Program presents a range of technology-based options for language programming that will help universities make more informed decisions about teaching less commonly taught languages. The eight chapters describe how different types of technologies are used to support language programs (i.e., Web, ITV, and audio- or video-based materials), discuss identifiable trends in e-language learning, and explore how technology addresses issues of equity, diversity, and opportunity. This book offers many lessons learned and decisions made as technology changes and learning needs become more complex. 188 pp.

2002   (SLTCC Technical Report #25) ISBN 0-8248-2634-5 $25.

AN INVESTIGATION OF SECOND LANGUAGE TASK-BASED PERFORMANCE ASSESSMENTS

JAMES DEAN BROWN, THOM HUDSON, JOHN M. NORRIS, & WILLIAM BONK

This volume describes the creation of performance assessment instruments and their validation (based on work started in TR# 18). It begins by explaining the test and rating scale development processes and the administration of the resulting three seven-task tests to 90 university level EFL and ESL students. The results are examined in terms of (a) the effects of test revision; (b) comparisons among the task-dependent, task-independent, and self-rating scales; and (c) reliability and validity issues. 240 pp.

2002   (SLTCC Technical Report #24) ISBN 0-8248-2633-7 $25.

MOTIVATION AND SECOND LANGUAGE ACQUISITION

ZOLTÁN DÖRNYEI
& RICHARD SCHMIDT
(Editors)

This volume — the second in this series concerned with motivation and foreign language learning — includes papers presented in a state-of-the-art colloquium on L2 motivation at the American Association for Applied Linguistics (Vancouver, 2000) and a number of specially commissioned studies. The 20 chapters, written by some of the best known researchers in the field, cover a wide range of theoretical and research methodological issues, and also offer empirical results (both qualitative and quantitative) concerning the learning of many different languages (Arabic, Chinese, English, Filipino, French, German, Hindi, Italian, Japanese, Russian, and Spanish) in a broad range of learning contexts (Bahrain, Brazil, Canada, Egypt, Finland, Hungary, Ireland, Israel, Japan, Spain, and the US). 520 pp.

2001 (SLTCC Technical Report #23) ISBN 0-8248-2458-X $25.

STUDIES ON KOREAN IN COMMUNITY SCHOOLS

DONG-JAE LEE,
SOOKEUN CHO,
MISEON LEE,
MINSUN SONG,
& WILLIAM O'GRADY
(Editors)

The papers in this volume focus on language teaching and learning in Korean community schools. Drawing on innovative experimental work and research in linguistics, education, and psychology, the contributors address issues of importance to teachers, administrators, and parents. Topics covered include childhood bilingualism, Korean grammar, language acquisition, children's literature, and language teaching methodology. 256 pp.

[in Korean]

2000 (SLTCC Technical Report #22) ISBN 0-8248-2352-4 $20.

A FOCUS ON LANGUAGE TEST DEVELOPMENT: EXPANDING THE LANGUAGE PROFICIENCY CONSTRUCT ACROSS A VARIETY OF TESTS

THOM HUDSON
& JAMES DEAN BROWN
(Editors)

This volume presents eight research studies that introduce a variety of novel, non-traditional forms of second and foreign language assessment. To the extent possible, the studies also show the entire test development process, warts and all. These language testing projects not only demonstrate many of the types of problems that test developers run into in the real world but also afford the reader unique insights into the language test development process. 230 pp.

2001 (SLTCC Technical Report #21) ISBN 0-8248-2351-6 $20.

A COMMUNICATIVE FRAMEWORK FOR INTRODUCTORY JAPANESE LANGUAGE CURRICULA

WASHINGTON STATE JAPANESE LANGUAGE CURRICULUM GUIDELINES COMMITTEE

2000

In recent years the number of schools offering Japanese nationwide has increased dramatically. Because of the tremendous popularity of Japanese language and the shortage of teachers, quite a few untrained, non-native and native teachers are in the classrooms and are expected to teach several levels of Japanese. These guidelines are intended to assist individual teachers and professional associations throughout the United States in designing Japanese language curricula. They are meant to serve as a framework from which language teaching can be expanded and are intended to allow teachers to enhance and strengthen the quality of Japanese language instruction. 168 pp.

(SLTCC Technical Report #20) ISBN 0–8248–2350–8 $20.

FOREIGN LANGUAGE TEACHING & MINORITY LANGUAGE EDUCATION

KATHRYN A. DAVIS
(Editor)

1999

This volume seeks to examine the potential for building relationships among foreign language, bilingual, and ESL programs towards fostering bilingualism. Part I of the volume examines the sociopolitical contexts for language partnerships, including:

- obstacles to developing bilingualism
- implications of acculturation, identity, and language issues for linguistic minorities.
- the potential for developing partnerships across primary, secondary, and tertiary institutions

Part II of the volume provides research findings on the *Foreign language partnership project* designed to capitalize on the resources of immigrant students to enhance foreign language learning. 152 pp.

(SLTCC Technical Report #19) ISBN 0–8248–2067–3 $20.

DESIGNING SECOND LANGUAGE PERFORMANCE ASSESSMENTS

JOHN M. NORRIS, JAMES DEAN BROWN, THOM HUDSON, & JIM YOSHIOKA

1998, 2000

This technical report focuses on the decision-making potential provided by second language performance assessments. The authors first situate performance assessment within a broader discussion of alternatives in language assessment and in educational assessment in general. They then discuss issues in performance assessment design, implementation, reliability, and validity. Finally, they present a prototype framework for second language performance assessment based on the integration of theoretical underpinnings and research findings from the task-based language teaching literature, the language testing literature, and the educational measurement literature. The authors outline test and item specifications, and they present numerous examples of prototypical language tasks. They also propose a research agenda focusing on the operationalization of second language performance assessments. 248 pp.

(SLTCC Technical Report #18) ISBN 0–8248–2109–2 $20.

SECOND LANGUAGE DEVELOPMENT IN WRITING: MEASURES OF FLUENCY, ACCURACY, & COMPLEXITY

KATE WOLFE-QUINTERO, SHUNJI INAGAKI, & HAE-YOUNG KIM

In this book, the authors analyze and compare the ways that fluency, accuracy, grammatical complexity, and lexical complexity have been measured in studies of language development in second language writing. More than 100 developmental measures are examined, with detailed comparisons of the results across the studies that have used each measure. The authors discuss the theoretical foundations for each type of developmental measure, and they consider the relationship between developmental measures and various types of proficiency measures. They also examine criteria for determining which developmental measures are the most successful, and suggest which measures are the most promising for continuing work on language development. 208 pp.

1998, 2002 (SLTCC Technical Report #17) ISBN 0-8248-2069-X $20.

THE DEVELOPMENT OF A LEXICAL TONE PHONOLOGY IN AMERICAN ADULT LEARNERS OF STANDARD MANDARIN CHINESE

SYLVIA HENEL SUN

The study reported is based on an assessment of three decades of research on the SLA of Mandarin tone. It investigates whether differences in learners' tone perception and production are related to differences in the effects of certain linguistic, task, and learner factors. The learners of focus are American students of Mandarin in Beijing, China. Their performances on two perception and three production tasks are analyzed through a host of variables and methods of quantification. 328 pp.

1998 (SLTCC Technical Report #16) ISBN 0-8248-2068-1 $20.

NEW TRENDS & ISSUES IN TEACHING JAPANESE LANGUAGE & CULTURE

HARUKO M. COOK, KYOKO HIJIRIDA, & MILDRED TAHARA (*Editors*)

In recent years, Japanese has become the fourth most commonly taught foreign language at the college level in the United States. As the number of students who study Japanese has increased, the teaching of Japanese as a foreign language has been established as an important academic field of study. This technical report includes nine contributions to the advancement of this field, encompassing the following five important issues:

- Literature and literature teaching
- Technology in the language classroom
- Orthography
- Testing
- Grammatical versus pragmatic approaches to language teaching

164 pp.

1997 (SLTCC Technical Report #15) ISBN 0-8248-2067-3 $20.

SIX MEASURES OF JSL PRAGMATICS

SAYOKO OKADA YAMASHITA

1996

This book investigates differences among tests that can be used to measure the cross-cultural pragmatic ability of English-speaking learners of Japanese. Building on the work of Hudson, Detmer, and Brown (Technical Reports #2 and #7 in this series), the author modified six test types which she used to gather data from North American learners of Japanese. She found numerous problems with the multiple-choice discourse completion test but reported that the other five tests all proved highly reliable and reasonably valid. Practical issues involved in creating and using such language tests are discussed from a variety of perspectives. 213 pp.

(SLTCC Technical Report #14) ISBN 0-8248-1914-4 $15.

LANGUAGE LEARNING STRATEGIES AROUND THE WORLD: CROSS-CULTURAL PERSPECTIVES

REBECCA L. OXFORD (Editor)

1996, 1997, 2002

Language learning strategies are the specific steps students take to improve their progress in learning a second or foreign language. Optimizing learning strategies improves language performance. This ground-breaking book presents new information about cultural influences on the use of language learning strategies. It also shows innovative ways to assess students' strategy use and remarkable techniques for helping students improve their choice of strategies, with the goal of peak language learning. 166 pp.

(SLTCC Technical Report #13) ISBN 0-8248-1910-1 $20.

TELECOLLABORATION IN FOREIGN LANGUAGE LEARNING: PROCEEDINGS OF THE HAWAI'I SYMPOSIUM

MARK WARSCHAUER (Editor)

1996

The Symposium on Local & Global Electronic Networking in Foreign Language Learning & Research, part of the National Foreign Language Resource Center's 1995 Summer Institute on Technology & the Human Factor in Foreign Language Education, included presentations of papers and hands-on workshops conducted by Symposium participants to facilitate the sharing of resources, ideas, and information about all aspects of electronic networking for foreign language teaching and research, including electronic discussion and conferencing, international cultural exchanges, real-time communication and simulations, research and resource retrieval via the Internet, and research using networks. This collection presents a sampling of those presentations. 252 pp.

(SLTCC Technical Report #12) ISBN 0-8248-1867-9 $20.

LANGUAGE LEARNING MOTIVATION: PATHWAYS TO THE NEW CENTURY

REBECCA L. OXFORD (Editor)

1996

This volume chronicles a revolution in our thinking about what makes students want to learn languages and what causes them to persist in that difficult and rewarding adventure. Topics in this book include the internal structures of and external connections with foreign language motivation; exploring adult language learning motivation, self-efficacy, and anxiety; comparing the motivations and learning strategies of students of Japanese and Spanish; and enhancing the theory of language learning motivation from many psychological and social perspectives. 218 pp.

(SLTCC Technical Report #11) ISBN 0-8248-1849-0 $20.

LINGUISTICS & LANGUAGE TEACHING: PROCEEDINGS OF THE SIXTH JOINT LSH-HATESL CONFERENCE

C. REVES,
C. STEELE,
& C. S. P. WONG
(Editors)

Technical Report #10 contains 18 articles revolving around the following three topics:
- Linguistic issues — These six papers discuss various linguistics issues: ideophones, syllabic nasals, linguistic areas, computation, tonal melody classification, and *wh*-words.
- Sociolinguistics — Sociolinguistic phenomena in Swahili, signing, Hawaiian, and Japanese are discussed in four of the papers.
- Language teaching and learning — These eight papers cover prosodic modification, note taking, planning in oral production, oral testing, language policy, L2 essay organization, access to dative alternation rules, and child noun phrase structure development. 364 pp.

1996 (SLTCC Technical Report #10) ISBN 0–8248–1851–2 $20.

ATTENTION & AWARENESS IN FOREIGN LANGUAGE LEARNING

RICHARD SCHMIDT
(Editor)

Issues related to the role of attention and awareness in learning lie at the heart of many theoretical and practical controversies in the foreign language field. This collection of papers presents research into the learning of Spanish, Japanese, Finnish, Hawaiian, and English as a second language (with additional comments and examples from French, German, and miniature artificial languages) that bear on these crucial questions for foreign language pedagogy. 394 pp.

1996 (SLTCC Technical Report #9) ISBN 0–8248–1794–X $20.

VIRTUAL CONNECTIONS: ONLINE ACTIVITIES & PROJECTS FOR NETWORKING LANGUAGE LEARNERS

MARK WARSCHAUER
(Editor)

Computer networking has created dramatic new possibilities for connecting language learners in a single classroom or across the globe. This collection of activities and projects makes use of e-mail, the internet, computer conferencing, and other forms of computer-mediated communication for the foreign and second language classroom at any level of instruction. Teachers from around the world submitted the activities compiled in this volume — activities that they have used successfully in their own classrooms. 417 pp.

1995, 1996 (SLTCC Technical Report #8) ISBN 0–8248–1793–1 $30.

DEVELOPING PROTOTYPIC MEASURES OF CROSS-CULTURAL PRAGMATICS

THOM HUDSON
EMILY DETMER
& J. D. BROWN

Although the study of cross-cultural pragmatics has gained importance in applied linguistics, there are no standard forms of assessment that might make research comparable across studies and languages. The present volume describes the process through which six forms of cross-cultural assessment were developed for second language learners of English. The models may be used for second language learners of other languages. The six forms of assessment involve two forms each of indirect discourse completion tests, oral language production, and self assessment. The procedures involve the assessment of requests, apologies, and refusals. 198 pp.

1995 (SLTCC Technical Report #7) ISBN 0–8248–1763–X $15.

THE ROLE OF PHONOLOGICAL CODING IN READING *KANJI*

SACHIKO MATSUNAGA

In this technical report, the author reports the results of a study that she conducted on phonological coding in reading *kanji* using an eye-movement monitor and draws some pedagogical implications. In addition, she reviews current literature on the different schools of thought regarding instruction in reading *kanji* and its role in the teaching of non-alphabetic written languages like Japanese. 64 pp.

1995 (SLTCC Technical Report #6) ISBN 0–8248–1734–6 $10.

PRAGMATICS OF CHINESE AS NATIVE & TARGET LANGUAGE

GABRIELE KASPER
(*Editor*)

This technical report includes six contributions to the study of the pragmatics of Mandarin Chinese:

- A report of an interview study conducted with nonnative speakers of Chinese; and
- Five data-based studies on the performance of different speech acts by native speakers of Mandarin — requesting, refusing, complaining, giving bad news, disagreeing, and complimenting.

312 pp.

1995 (SLTCC Technical Report #5) ISBN 0–8248–1733–8 $15.

A BIBLIOGRAPHY OF PEDAGOGY & RESEARCH IN INTERPRETATION & TRANSLATION

ETILVIA ARJONA

This technical report includes four types of bibliographic information on translation and interpretation studies:

- Research efforts across disciplinary boundaries — cognitive psychology, neurolinguistics, psycholinguistics, sociolinguistics, computational linguistics, measurement, aptitude testing, language policy, decision-making, theses, dissertations;
- Training information covering — program design, curriculum studies, instruction, school administration;
- Instruction information detailing — course syllabi, methodology, models, available textbooks; and
- Testing information about aptitude, selection, diagnostic tests.

115 pp.

1993 (SLTCC Technical Report #4) ISBN 0–8248–1572–6 $10.

PRAGMATICS OF JAPANESE AS NATIVE & TARGET LANGUAGE

GABRIELE KASPER
(*Editor*)

This technical report includes three contributions to the study of the pragmatics of Japanese:

- A bibliography on speech act performance, discourse management, and other pragmatic and sociolinguistic features of Japanese;
- A study on introspective methods in examining Japanese learners' performance of refusals; and
- A longitudinal investigation of the acquisition of the particle *ne* by nonnative speakers of Japanese.

125 pp.

1992, 1996 (SLTCC Technical Report #3) ISBN 0–8248–1462–2 $10.

A FRAMEWORK FOR TESTING CROSS-CULTURAL PRAGMATICS

THOM HUDSON, EMILY DETMER & J. D. BROWN

This technical report presents a framework for developing methods that assess cross-cultural pragmatic ability. Although the framework has been designed for Japanese and American cross-cultural contrasts, it can serve as a generic approach that can be applied to other language contrasts. The focus is on the variables of social distance, relative power, and the degree of imposition within the speech acts of requests, refusals, and apologies. Evaluation of performance is based on recognition of the speech act, amount of speech, forms or formulæ used, directness, formality, and politeness. 51 pp.

1992 (SLTCC Technical Report #2)   ISBN 0–8248–1463–0 $10.

RESEARCH METHODS IN INTERLANGUAGE PRAGMATICS

GABRIELE KASPER & MERETE DAHL

This technical report reviews the methods of data collection employed in 39 studies of interlanguage pragmatics, defined narrowly as the investigation of nonnative speakers' comprehension and production of speech acts, and the acquisition of L2-related speech act knowledge. Data collection instruments are distinguished according to the degree to which they constrain informants' responses, and whether they tap speech act perception/comprehension or production. A main focus of discussion is the validity of different types of data, in particular their adequacy to approximate authentic performance of linguistic action. 51 pp.

1991 (SLTCC Technical Report #1)   ISBN 0–8248–1419–3 $10.

Stafford Library
Columbia College
1001 Rogers Street
Columbia, Missouri 65216